Teaching the
Tough Issues

Teaching the Tough Issues

Problem Solving from Multiple Perspectives
in Middle and High School Humanities Classes

Jacqueline Darvin

Foreword by
Douglas Fisher

TEACHERS COLLEGE PRESS

TEACHERS COLLEGE | COLUMBIA UNIVERSITY
NEW YORK AND LONDON

Published by Teachers College Press, 1234 Amsterdam Avenue, New York, NY 10027

Copyright © 2015 by Teachers College, Columbia University

The graphic organizers, and the art featured in them, were created using Inspiration® 9, a product of Inspiration Software, Inc.

Library of Congress Cataloging-in-Publication Data is available at loc.gov

ISBN 978-0-8077-5653-9 (paperback)
ISBN 978-0-8077-5654-6 (hardcover)
ISBN 978-0-8077-7378-9 (ebook)

Printed on acid-free paper
Manufactured in the United States of America

22 21 20 19 18 17 16 15   8 7 6 5 4 3 2 1

To the teachers of New York City and everywhere who have the foresight and courage to teach the tough issues. Your bravery and dedication are beyond measure. Thank you.

Contents

Foreword

Awkward. In a word, that's what this book is about, or rather it's what this book addresses. We've all had those awkward situations in class when we know that we need to respond, but we're not sure how. Typically, the awkward situation arises from something a student says. At that moment, it's as if E. F. Hutton is ready to speak—everyone listens. The room is eerily silent and all eyes are fixated on the teacher, anticipating a response. In the past 30 days, I have been asked if the characters in *The Fault in Our Stars* (Green, 2012) had sex, and if they did, how did Hazel Grace breathe; if I believed in God, and if God could be made up, like Jason did in the book *Godless* (Hautman, 2004); and if I thought we should rename diseases, conditions, and procedures that were originally named after Nazi scientists, such as Wegener's granulomatosis.

These moments are awkward because we're unsure how to respond. We ask ourselves a multitude of questions, such as "Will I lose my job if I respond in one way or the other?" "Will we unduly influence young minds as we try to clarify our thinking on complex social issues?" and "What do I think about that issue?"

In response, teachers often refuse to answer, or worse, punish students for asking questions. What I've learned about adolescents in the past 20 years is that they have questions, questions that they really want to find answers to. And, if they respect their teachers, they want to know what their teachers think about those same questions. At the school where I work, we have organized our curriculum around essential questions that the students nominate and vote on. The adults in the school get no vote on these essential questions. And they ask questions that allow us to explore a wide range of topics and ideas. For example, recent questions that we've investigated as a school include:

- How does where you live influence how you live?
- Do you avenge or forgive?
- Can you buy your way to happiness?
- Does gender matter?
- What sets your heart on fire?
- What does #YOLO mean to you?

Our students read a lot of different texts and interview people about their perspectives, and then write an essay in which they answer the question using the sources they've collected and analyzed, as well as their new understanding of their own thinking. For example, Elizabeth, one of my students, wrote an essay over 1,000 words in length, in response to the question about where you live, based on her reading of two texts that explored the Vietnam War, as well as interviews of people in our community. An excerpt from Elizabeth's writing demonstrates her thinking and understanding of one of the texts:

In the novel *The Things They Carried*, the characters are introduced as kids, some fresh out of high school or college. But they were soon changed into hardened men who had to kill just to keep their "manly" image. O'Brien (1990) says, "Men killed, and died, because they were embarrassed not to." The main character, Lieutenant Cross, was just a boy lost in love when he arrived in Vietnam. But as soon as one of his men was shot and killed under his command, he lost it. "They marched into the village of Than Khe. They burned everything. They shot chickens and dogs, they trashed the village well, they called in artillery and watched the wreckage, then they marched for several hours through the hot afternoon, and then at dusk, while Kiowa explained how Lavender died, Lieutenant Cross found himself trembling." The pressure of living in a warzone dramatically changed Lieutenant Cross. In this case, where he lived impacted how he lived.

I thought that we were doing a pretty good job with inviting students into critical conversations about ideas that matter to them. But having read Jacqueline Darvin's book *Teaching the Tough Issues: Problem Solving from Multiple Perspectives in Middle and High School Humanities Classes* made me realize that I had some room to grow. At our school, we have the hard conversations that students want to have, but we don't actively pursue deep and meaningful conversations that allow for those awkward moments to arise. We react to students' inquiry rather than provoke it. Darvin gave me, and my colleagues, a way to change that. The Cultural and Political Vignettes (CPVs as she calls them) can be easily used to facilitate conversations around tough issues and provide expert guidance for teachers to navigate ebb and flow of these interactions in their classrooms. Having tried them on a few of these with my own students, I am pleased to report that they felt empowered, valued, and respected when we engaged in these topics that matter so much to them. Adolescence is a time when we figure out who we are and what we believe. Darvin has provided us all with a powerful tool for guiding students as they explore their identity, unafraid to explore what it means to be human. Further, she has provided educators with the confidence needed to steer, rather than squelch, discussions about controversial issues in the classroom. CPVs allow awkward silences to become reflective moments. Enjoy.

Douglas Fisher

Acknowledgments

Without the middle and high school teachers from New York City and Long Island whose work is featured in the chapters ahead, this book would have never been possible. The majority of the contributing teachers are English and social studies teachers in the New York metropolitan area, who were graduate students in the Literacy 5–12 Master's Program at Queens College of the City University of New York from 2005 to the present. They are wonderful, creative educators who are teaching the tough issues in their humanities classes each and every day, and they and their secondary students are the inspiration for everything I do—my teaching, my scholarship, and my going to work each day. Their bravery and dedication, in spite of enormous challenges, make me truly proud to be a teacher educator.

It was Dr. Eleanor Armour-Thomas, my mentor and the chair of the Secondary Education and Youth Services Department at Queens College, who encouraged me to write my first single-authored book. She read many drafts of this manuscript, always lending valuable words of encouragement and constructive critique. Drs. Alice Artzt and Bobbie Kabuto at Queens College also gave me thoughtful feedback on rough drafts and assisted me with my academic writing. It is very important to have colleagues who care, and I thank them sincerely for their time.

At Teachers College Press, my editor Emily Spangler deserves a special thank you. Her developmental edits and suggested revisions truly transformed what was once a very rough manuscript into a polished finished product of which I am very proud. Emily is easy to work with, fair, knowledgeable, and prompt. I couldn't have asked for a better editor.

I would like to express my gratitude to Dr. Douglas Fisher for graciously writing the Foreword for this book. Dr. Fisher is a professor of Educational Leadership at San Diego State University and a wonderful, prolific scholar. He is not afraid to teach the tough issues, and his work has been highly inspirational to me throughout the course of my career.

I would also like to thank Inspiration Software for granting me permission to include figures in this book that were created using their amazing software. Inspiration is a great resource for teachers and students for creating all kinds of graphic organizers, and I highly recommend it.

Finally, I want to express gratitude to my parents, Barbara and Bill, and my brother, Greg, for their constant encouragement and patience with me through this time-consuming and rewarding process. You can all finally stop asking me when I will be finished with the book.

Introduction

Every teacher has encountered situations in which class discussion takes a sudden, uncomfortable turn. One such situation occurred for me when I was a novice teacher, standing in front of a high school English class. We were studying *Billy Budd, Sailor,* the 1924 Herman Melville classic tale of a sailor who is falsely accused of conspiracy to commit mutiny and executed, when one of my 11th-grade students called out, "Was Melville gay or something? This book seems so gay to me." Several students giggled, others put their heads down or looked away uncomfortably, while most stared directly at me, eagerly awaiting my reaction and response.

For what seemed like an eternity, even though it was only about 30 seconds, I said absolutely nothing. My face reddened as I struggled for words to address this student. I knew from my background in English literature that there were homosexual references and undertones in the story and that countless literary critics assumed from his writings that Melville was conflicted about his sexual identity, but standing in front of that class in 1992, I admit I was at a complete loss for how to discuss this topic thoughtfully and appropriately with a group of 16-year-olds.

THE NEED FOR CPVS IN SECONDARY CLASSROOMS

Although my teacher preparation program had given me the ability to write decent lesson plans and demonstrate effective classroom management, my training did not cover how to address culturally and politically sensitive issues such as sexual preference with a group of high school students. I knew that anything I said could be misconstrued or misinterpreted by my students, their parents, and administrators and that I was, in effect, facing a political minefield by discussing sexual preference in class. As I stood there speechless, conflicting thoughts and questions raced through my mind: What if I have gay students in the class who would be embarrassed by this discussion? What if I have gay students in the class who desperately want and need their teacher to address this issue? What if I have students from strict religious backgrounds who would be upset by this discussion? What would parents say about my discussing this subject in class? What would my administrator think? And so forth.

I don't remember the exact words I used to respond to my student that day, but I do remember basically sweeping his question under the rug and redirecting

1

the conversation elsewhere because I was too uncomfortable and lacked the peda-gogical tools to address the issue intelligently. I felt, even then, that I was doing my students a terrible disservice by choosing not to discuss something that was central to both the theme of the work and the author's life and could be related to serious issues of identity with which some of the class members might be struggling. I had read about increased drug and alcohol abuse among gay teens and knew that they committed suicide at a much higher rate than straight teens. I had circumvented a topic that was essential not only to the work we were reading but to the lives of the students and the shaping of their perceptions about sexuality and, even more subtly, what constitutes "appropriate" discussion in a high school English class. I knew that in the future, to be the kind of teacher that I wanted to be, I had to find ways of teaching the tough issues in my classroom. I didn't know then that this theme of finding ways for teachers to better address culturally and politically sensitive issues with students would be one that would later become central to my research and work as a teacher educator.

WHAT ARE CULTURAL AND POLITICAL VIGNETTES (CPVS)?

Although most teachers know the content that they teach and how to develop lesson plans, and have some command of classroom management, few teachers feel comfortable and confident facilitating conversations about culturally and po-litically controversial and sensitive issues with their students in ways that honor the students' diverse voices and lead to critical, transformative thinking and, more important, action. One of the greatest challenges facing teachers today involves working in culturally and linguistically diverse settings. Although much has been written about this challenge and its impact on the field of teacher education (Ben-Peretz, 2001; Cochran-Smith, 2005; Darvin, 2010, 2012; Hoffman & Pearson, 2000; Ladson-Billings, 1995), the majority of the research in this area has focused on the attitudes and lack of knowledge of preservice teachers, not on pedagogical prac-tices that help teachers be successful (Darvin, 2011a, 2011b, 2011c; Sleeter, 2001).

In short, although there are countless pedagogical processes and teaching strategies available to teachers, few are designed to facilitate higher-level think-ing, problem posing, problem solving, and reading, writing, talking, and listening about culturally and politically complex and controversial issues. This book pres-ents a pedagogical model that can help secondary teachers to meet these import-ant but often overlooked goals with their students, while concurrently assisting them in addressing the Common Core State Standards (CCSS) and other curric-ular directives.

In this book, I describe a series of pedagogical practices or processes that I have termed Cultural and Political Vignettes (CPVs). I have chosen the word "vi-gnette" because CPVs encompass aspects of all of the definitions for vignettes, but also stretch the meaning a bit to describe something new. Vignettes are short, descriptive, graceful, and powerful literary sketches, accounts, scenes, episodes, or snapshots that focus on one moment and/or give an impression of a character, idea, setting, or object and evoke emotion from the respondent.

The pedagogical processes described in this book are termed Cultural and Political Vignettes because cultural and/or political variables must be taken into account by both the CPV creators and respondents. Although we often think of vignettes as being very brief, and the term sometimes connotes a delightful flight of fancy, I use it here to refer to more involved examples that often reference very serious subject matter. Rather than sticking to the traditional meanings or definitions of vignettes, CPVs expand on them to include more developed storylines and details than those normally associated with the term.

CPVs are potential cultural and/or political situations, real or imagined, that are presented to students so they can practice the complex decisionmaking skills they need in today's diverse classrooms, schools, and communities. They invite students to engage in dialogue, problem pose, and problem-solve through the use of controversial issues that they need to evaluate critically and view through multiple perspectives or lenses. CPVs can be used as part of prereading, or during reading and postreading and writing activities. They are designed to aid students in both developing their own viewpoints on critical, contentious issues and actively listening to and critiquing the viewpoints of others.

CPVs often deal with the kinds of sensitive cultural and political issues that teachers identify as being the most uncomfortable to address with their students, such as race, class, gender, ethnicity, sex, sexual preference, bullying, and politics, to name a few. They are designed to ask students to reflect on and talk about their values, ideologies, biases, philosophies, and actions.

CPVs ask students to consider problematic situations and to practice or rehearse the thought processes involved in addressing the problems at hand, so that when they are later confronted with similar situations in real life, they have virtual or simulated problem-solving experiences on which to base their decisions and actions. CPVs can be used by secondary teachers of any content area, but they are particularly useful in middle and high school humanities classes. CPVs are flexible. Teachers can adjust them to the interests, needs, and skills of their students, and design them to address classroom content or social issues that their students encounter. CPVs invite teachers to create organic, context-specific, situated activities for their classrooms that enable their students to discuss, read, write, listen, and role-play about difficult topics.

CPVs are designed to influence not only students' thinking about CPV topics but their subsequent actions as well. CPVs ask students to practice and refine complex communication skills and to do so in ways that make sense in the context of authentic situations that occur in real life. Although many teachers have used techniques such as role-playing to address difficult or controversial issues, CPVs offer opportunities that go beyond the scope and sequence of traditional role-plays. The dialogue that occurs before, during, and after the CPV activities and the ways in which the CPVs emerge from the classroom contexts are just a few of the elements that set them apart from similar methods.

CPVs can fulfill many curricular functions and are appropriate in a wide range of classroom contexts. In some instances, CPVs are used to explore cultural differences and/or controversial social issues, such as homophobia or racism. In other instances, a CPV topic might be sensitive, rather than controversial, and deal with the various political nuances of a situation. On other occasions, CPVs can be used to meet behavioral objectives with students. I have termed these "behavioral" CPVs because they deal specifically with behavioral goals that contribute to students' academic success. Behavioral CPVs can be designed, for example, to improve students' abilities in working cooperatively with one another, to help them learn to become better active listeners, or to teach them how to be more effective public speakers.

Other CPVs relate directly to course content. I have termed these "content-driven" CPVs because they are linked to particular content objectives and course texts. Finally, in some cases CPV topics might not be at all controversial or problematic but used primarily to help respondents practice problem solving from multiple perspectives. Examples are CPVs that ask students to consider large, overarching themes that are present in literary works and informational texts, such as honesty, friendship, or overcoming adversity.

In short, there are many ways in which CPVs can work to illuminate different perspectives, and that they can be used in such various ways is a testament to their flexibility and usefulness across contexts, grade levels, and ability levels.

THE BIRTH OF CPVS AS A PEDAGOGICAL STRATEGY

My first in-class CPV-related activity occurred by complete accident. We were reading Sonia Nieto's book *The Light in Their Eyes: Creating Multicultural Learning Communities* (1999), a text I use in an undergraduate education course that I teach at Queens College called Language, Literacy and Culture in Education. In the book, Nieto posed a "cultural problem" to her students, who, like mine, were preservice teachers:

> A new student from India comes to your school and on her first day in the cafeteria, she begins eating rice with her hands. Several of the children make fun of her. You are her teacher and you happen to be in the lunchroom when this happens. What do you do? (Nieto, 1999, p. 74)

When I posed Nieto's "cultural problem" to my own students and asked them to respond to it in writing, I was pleasantly surprised by the range of responses that I received and even more intrigued by the enthusiasm of the verbal class debate that ensued. An apparently simple situation such as this cultural problem inspired an intricate dialogue that revealed the students' increasing awareness of the convoluted system of cultural, political, and social forces that intersect in schools. Immediately, my class became divided over whether the teacher on lunch duty in the cafeteria should intervene. Additionally, the students' suggested interventions and the rationales behind them differed dramatically. Some students believed that it was a teacher's responsibility to intervene and protect the Indian girl from the other students' taunting, citing tragedies like the school shootings that occurred in Columbine, Colorado, as a result of bullying that was ignored by faculty. Others emphatically argued that the teacher would only make the situation worse for the girl by calling more attention to her and making her feel that her cultural values and Indian customs were not respected by the school and faculty.

As the class dialogue continued to evolve, this cultural problem took on even more of a life of its own and was divided into two separate issues by the students. The first question became whether and/or how the teacher should address the girl. The second was whether and/or how to address the mob of children making fun of her. Several students recommended that the teacher act as sociocultural mediator and talk with the Indian girl about American ways of eating, while still transmitting respect toward her way of eating rice and allowing the girl to decide whether she wanted to reject or retain this aspect of her culture. Other students suggested that the teacher should use this event as a springboard for a lesson about cultural differences in eating habits and that the students would make the connections themselves without the teacher needing to call attention to the teasing that had occurred in the lunchroom. Others advocated that the teacher should sit down at the same table as the child and start eating rice (or some American finger food, such as fries, pizza, or a burger) with his or her hands to quietly demonstrate that eating with one's hands is acceptable.

Regardless of the ways in which my students first responded to Nieto's cultural problem, the majority changed or broadened their responses as a result of the sharing and discussion that followed. We later revisited the cultural problem after we completed Nieto's text, and by that point in the course, the students' viewpoints had evolved even further as a result of reading the text and engaging in the accompanying class discussions. I learned that day how important it was for me, as the facilitator, to make it clear to the students that there were no completely right or wrong solutions to the problem, and that all opinions represented reasonable approaches that someone might take in the situation. Many students became visibly frustrated by the cultural problem because they walked away with more questions than answers. It is this very feeling of disequilibrium that is effective in making CPVs powerful because it closely mirrors the feeling that people have in real life when confronted by complex problems.

CPVs were first introduced into secondary classrooms as part of a homework assignment in which I asked my students, who are middle and high school teachers, to create CPVs for use with their own students. As part of this assignment, they collected and shared several of their students' responses to their CPVs and wrote brief reflections on whether they believed the CPV was effective in helping them to address a culturally or politically sensitive topic with their students. The class discussion that resulted from this homework assignment was the first indication that CPVs could be positively utilized in secondary classrooms due to their versatility and, in particular, their strong connections to the tenets of critical literacy.

A CPV EVENT IN A SECONDARY SOCIAL STUDIES CLASSROOM

An example that illustrates some of the details of the CPV strategy in a secondary social studies class occurred in an ethnically diverse New York City public school comprised of predominantly African American, West Indian, and Latino students, with small percentages of Caucasian and Asian students. In this 8th-grade American History unit, the teacher wanted to determine how much prior knowledge his students had retained from their 6th-grade lessons on slavery in the United States and also whether they would make any thematic connections to lessons they had learned in 7th grade about the Holocaust. He also wanted to introduce the concepts of empathy and apathy to his students and talk about times throughout history when people have acted courageously or remained detached from helping others who are being violently oppressed and victimized in their midst.

Prior to being presented with the CPV, the students had just read about and discussed the Fugitive Slave Act, as well as excerpts from Harriet Beecher Stowe's classic work *Uncle Tom's Cabin* (1852/1878). To help assess his students' prior and evolving knowledge about American slavery and to provide a writing prompt that could introduce the concepts of empathy and apathy, the teacher provided the following CPV prompt to his 8th-grade students:

> Imagine that you are a white Northerner and a runaway slave from the South knocks on your door in the middle of the night. He asks you to hide him. You are aware of the Fugitive Slave Act, and you know that if a police officer knocks on your door and finds the runaway slave, you will be held responsible and your consequence will be jail time and a harsh fine. You have your own family with two children. What would you do? (Darvin, 2011d, p. 10)

In response to this CPV prompt, one student wrote:

If I was a white Northerner and this happened, I would not hide the runaway slave, even if I wanted to because doing that would be illegal and could put my family and children in danger. If I had no family or kids, I might take a chance and try and help the slave. Even though I disagree with runaway slaves being returned to their masters, I would have to find another way to try and help them that didn't break the law and put me and my family in trouble. Back then, the Abolitionists (that was the name of the people who wanted slavery to stop) like me nicknamed the Fugitive Slave Act the "Bloodhound Law" because they used to use dogs to go after the runaway slaves and bite them. What was really bad, too, was that the slave had no rights, and the slave owners didn't even have to have any proof that they owned the slave, like a paper or whatever. It was their word against the slave's, and they could say they owned him, even if they didn't. It was really wrong.

A second student responded:

I would go ahead and hide that slave anyway. It's like the same thing we learned about the Christians and priests who hid Jewish kids during World War II. They didn't care if Hitler came after them because they were on the right side. Sometimes, you have to take a chance to do the right thing for another person, even if it could be dangerous for you. That's the only way things ever change. The Fugitive Slave Law was a bad law, so people shouldn't follow it. They had to go against it so it could get changed, which it did later on.

As seen in these students' responses, the CPV prompt provided the teacher with windows into the students' background knowledge concerning slavery and, in particular, the Fugitive Slave Act. They also provided opportunities for him to introduce the concepts of empathy and apathy, which he did during the class discussion, and allowed his students to further explain why their responses demonstrated empathy or required apathy (in this case, to avoid risking harm to their own families). At the conclusion of the 2-day lesson on the Fugitive Slave Act, students were asked to write culminating persuasive essays in which they defended or refuted the Fugitive Slave Act and provided textual evidence from both the law itself and *Uncle Tom's Cabin* to support their positions. The CPV prompt served as an entry point for the discussion, after which the teacher directed the students to additional texts that could help them prepare their position papers.

The texts presented to the students following their initial responses to the CPV included replicas of actual posters from 1851 warning the "Colored people of Boston" about policemen acting as slave catchers, political cartoons from the era that were used as propaganda, and an excerpt from *I've Got a Home in Glory Land: A Lost Tale of the Underground Railroad* (Frost, 2007). In addition to the curricular goals that the CPV helped the teacher to address, more general goals regarding students' interpersonal communication skills were also highlighted in the conversation that followed the students responding to and sharing their CPV responses verbally with their classmates.

The following excerpt illustrates the teacher in the middle of the CPV event as he effectively mediates students' thoughts and language:

William: I'm not sure if this has to do with the CPV, but I feel like the whole slavery thing is played out. I mean, it happened a real long time ago, but there are people still talking about it like it happened last week. I think we need to move on and stop talking about it.

Mr. Roberts: Does anyone want to respond to this comment?

Juana: I agree. I am tired of it, too. My dad says that Black people in this country still use slavery as an excuse to do bad in school and steal and be on welfare and stuff. My parents came here from Colombia, a really poor country, and they have good jobs and a nice house. My dad says most Black people are just lazy and use slavery as an excuse not to work hard like my parents.

Mr. Roberts: Thank you for sharing your dad's opinion, but please be careful about discussing racial stereotypes. We do not want to offend people in our class or make racist comments. Are there other opinions on this issue?

Tiffany: My parents say that, too, but I don't think Black people are lazy. My baseball coach is Black, and he is not lazy at all.

Mr. Roberts: We are getting off track here. We are discussing our responses to our CPV about slavery and whether or not slavery is an issue that we should be learning about in our class. Let's try not to use stereotypes or talk about individual people that we know. Would anyone like to please respond to William's original comment that we should move on and not talk about slavery anymore?

William: I'm just saying, why are we still talking about slavery? All it does is make people feel bad. Black people even call themselves the N word now.

Mr. Roberts: Can you explain what you mean by that please?

William: I mean Black people feel bad about it because their relatives were slaves, and White people feel bad about it because their relatives were the ones who made the Black people slaves. It would be better to just forget about it and move on. And if Black people can call themselves the N word, then it shows they don't care.

Malik: I disagree. If we don't learn about it and talk about it, then maybe it could happen again. And the N word is still a bad word. Rappers use it, but regular Black people don't, and if you call a Black person the N word, that's still very disrespectful!

Mr. Roberts: Okay, so we are now talking about two different issues. The first point that William made is that people, both Black and White, feel bad when we talk about slavery, and the second point he made was that if Black people use the N word, it means that they don't care about the history behind it. Any thoughts?

Malik: I don't use the N word because it's not nice and hurts people.

Tiffany: If Black people want to use it, they can, but people who aren't Black shouldn't say it.

Mr. Roberts: You guys are so smart. You are talking about an issue that is very controversial. A lot of adults, Black and those from other races, disagree on whether or not the N word should be used today, by whom, and when. One of the things to think about, though, is how language like that makes people *feel*.

Crystal: I think it's *good* that Black and White people feel bad when we talk about slavery. We should learn about it in school because it was a terrible thing, and feeling bad about it helps us remember how bad it was so we don't do it again. I'm Black, and I *never* use the N word. My mom says that Black people died over that word, and my brothers and I are not allowed to say it. *Ever.*

Mr. Roberts: Okay, Crystal has just shared a different perspective with us. She disagrees with William because she thinks that we *do* need to learn about and remember slavery. There is an old saying, "Those who forget history are condemned to repeat it." Please write this quote at the top of a clean page in your response journals. For homework, please write a paragraph about what you think this quote means in your own words and a second paragraph on your reactions to the slavery CPV discussion that we just had in class today. Thank you for sharing your important ideas respectfully with the class. Great job!

As seen in this excerpt, the teacher made a concerted effort to honor all of the students' voices and opinions, but ensured that they expressed themselves in ways that were appropriate and respectful. When the discussion began to go off track, the teacher redirected that student back to the original discussion topic of slavery and whether it should be taught today. He cautioned the students to avoid stereotypes and discussing individual people they know. At several points in the class discussion, he summarized the students' main points and then asked for additional input from class members who had not yet contributed to the conversation. When the students began discussing the use of the "N word," the teacher did not shy away from the topic or shut the conversation down, as many teachers would have done in this situation. Instead, he used the opportunity as a teachable moment to praise his students for bringing up a subtopic that is clearly controversial, even among adults. He also encouraged students to "think about how language like that makes people *feel*."

Because the teacher had created a classroom environment that was thoughtful and civil, students were not inhibited or afraid to express themselves. The teacher told me that the students couldn't have had this discussion at the beginning of the school year; it had taken some time and practice for the students to become comfortable with expressing their ideas and opinions. In the beginning, when he first started using CPVs in his class, many students were reticent to share their responses with the class. Eighth grade is a time when adolescents are particularly worried about what their peers think about them, and teenagers often avoid being spotlighted during class conversations in front of their friends. He explained that once students realized that there weren't right or wrong answers and that everyone had valuable contributions to add to the conversation, they began to slowly open up.

This teacher also mentioned that, early on, he often had to stop students from laughing inappropriately, talking while others were talking, and making off-color or silly remarks. One technique he used was to gently ring a small replica of the Liberty Bell that he kept on his desk, signaling that students needed to stop laughing and talking. He told students that the Liberty Bell was a symbol of freedom, and that when he rang it, it meant that some students were being disrespectful to one of their classmates and negatively affecting that person's freedom to express himself or herself to a respectful audience. He also had to find ways to elicit responses from students in the class who were less vocal and willing to share. One strategy he used was to pass a microphone around the room and require that every student in the class make at least one contribution to the discussion in order for them to receive participation points for that day's class.

Also, at the start of the school year, this teacher selected students who had strong communication skills to model a respectful conversation about a CPV theme in front of the entire class. He believed that this "fishbowl" modeling activity was helpful in allowing students to witness what a respectful dialogue looks like and to better internalize the process. The fishbowl method is described in greater detail in Chapter 1.

When I inquired about the homework assignment, the teacher explained that it had grown organically from the students' conversation, and that he hadn't planned it. He said that this often happened when he was using the CPV strategy, and that he believed that because the homework assignment came from the students' own thoughts and conversation they were more motivated to complete the assignment than if he had given them a teacher-made homework assignment.

Summing up his feelings about using the CPV strategy in his 8th-grade social studies class, the teacher reported:

Middle school students go through many difficult changes, and it is essential that they develop the skills that they need to make the best decisions during this crucial point in their development. In my view, the CPV strategy serves two important and related purposes: The first is that it hooks the students and provides motivation for learning, and the second is that it allows them to practice their problem-solving and communication skills around sensitive topics.

THE ROLE OF CPVS IN SECONDARY ARTS, LITERATURE, AND HISTORY

In the 1970s, Simon, Howe, and Kirschenbaum created what they termed the "values clarification" approach. They wrote a classic book in which teachers were presented with 79 detailed strategies to help students build seven "valuing processes" into their lives. The seven subprocesses of valuing identified in the book were (1) prizing and cherishing one's beliefs and behaviors; (2) publicly affirming, when appropriate; (3) choosing from alternatives; (4) choosing after consideration of consequences; (5) choosing freely; (6) acting on one's beliefs; and (7) acting with a pattern, consistency, and repetition (Simon et al., 1978). The authors noted, even back then, that rarely in school curricula is attention given to the examination of values, ideas, and goals, even though the value systems that students develop are directly related to the kind of citizens they will become. The goals of the values clarification strategies were to involve students in practical experiences, make them aware of their own feelings, ideas, and beliefs, and help them to make conscious and deliberate choices and decisions, based on their clarified value systems.

The Values Clarification Approach is still relevant and influential today, particularly for educators and school counselors concerned with helping students to clarify their own belief systems, without judgment or moralizing. Simon et al. republished their seminal book in 2009, and their work has also been revisited and expanded upon more recently by other scholars who are interested in values education, including Toomey & Clement's *International Research Handbook on Values Education and Student Wellbeing* (2010) and Straughtan's (2012) book, *Can We Teach Children to Be Good? Basic Issues in Moral, Personal and Social Education.*

The CPV model shares Simon and colleagues' goals with regard to values clarification but does so in a more flexible, modern way that encourages teachers and students to create their own prompts, based on their own particular problem-posing, curricular, and behavioral goals. It is only through confronting controversial topics head-on and doing so in ways that honor students' diverse opinions in a safe environment that secondary students will see relevance between the controversial issues discussed in arts and humanities courses and their own lives. CPVs play an important role in the teaching of the arts, literature, and history by providing opportunities for secondary teachers and students to explore themselves and others and, in doing this, become more culturally and politically sensitive and aware citizens.

Closely related to the body of work on values clarification is the popular movement in education today of teaching for social justice (Adams, Bell, & Griffin, 2007; Bell, 2010; Christensen, 2000; Kumashiro, 2009; Shor, 2012; Winn, 2011). In my view, teaching for social justice always involves attempting to right some kind of wrong or to teach in ways that reveal social injustices to students and invite them to problem-solve and create possible solutions to help alleviate these injustices. Teaching for social justice is closely related to values clarification because as students clarify their value systems and dialogue about their beliefs, it is a natural progression for them to take greater interest in the social issues that surround them in their school and communities and want to correct injustices. Linda Christensen, in her classic book *Reading, Writing, and Rising Up: Teaching about Social Justice and the Power of the Written Word* (2000), writes about reading and writing as emancipatory acts. She believes in the Freirian ideal that when students are taught to read "the word and the world" (Freire & Macedo, 2013), then their minds become unshackled and they will seek to use their literacy skills to challenge social injustices and create a better world.

You will see as you read through the classroom examples offered throughout this book that the teachers profiled use CPVs proactively to achieve their teaching goals and to engage their students in difficult discussions around real-life issues occurring in their schools and communities. Some of the tough issues that are addressed in the following chapters include substance abuse, sexual assault, suicide, slavery, divorce, and mental illness. A comprehensive directory of all the CPVs featured throughout the book appears in the appendix at the conclusion of the text.

CHAPTER 1

The Four CPV Stages and How CPVs Help Teachers to Realize the Common Core State Standards (CCSS)

As depicted in Figure 1.1, the implementation of CPVs is done in four stages. It is a four-stage model for several compelling reasons, the most important of which is that it is a gradual release of responsibility pedagogical model. Gradual release models of instruction are ones in which over time, teaching and learning become more and more student directed, and students take on greater control over and responsibility for their academic tasks and achievements. The teacher takes on facilitating and consulting roles, while students become more adept at managing and directing their own learning tasks. Responsibilities are gradually released from the teacher to the students over time, as students become more comfortable and confident with the content they are learning and the pedagogical practices that are being employed. Proponents of gradual release models (Fisher & Frey, 2003, 2013; Israel & Massey, 2005; Pearson & Gallagher, 1983) believe that they are effective in teaching students how to be self-directed learners and giving them the academic skills they will need to be successful in college and their future careers, a primary goal of the CCSS and many other learning standards and directives.

CPV IMPLEMENTATION AS A FOUR-STAGE CURRICULAR MODEL

Stage 1, the stage during which students respond to teacher-created CPVs verbally and in writing, is the first level of CPV implementation (see Figure 1.1). Beginning with teacher-created CPVs enables students to become more at ease with a pedagogical strategy with which they are not familiar and allows them to increase their comfort levels with CPVs slowly. During this initial stage, students are given a lot of time to formulate their verbal or written responses, and they may choose to share or not share particular aspects of their responses with classmates. Because this stage often occurs at the beginning of the school year, when students might not know their teachers or classmates well, it gives them time to become more familiar with one another and to increase their risk taking with regard to sharing their views on politically and culturally controversial and sensitive issues slowly. Some teachers won't find their students ready for or receptive to CPVs right

Figure 1.1. The Four Stages of CPV Implementation

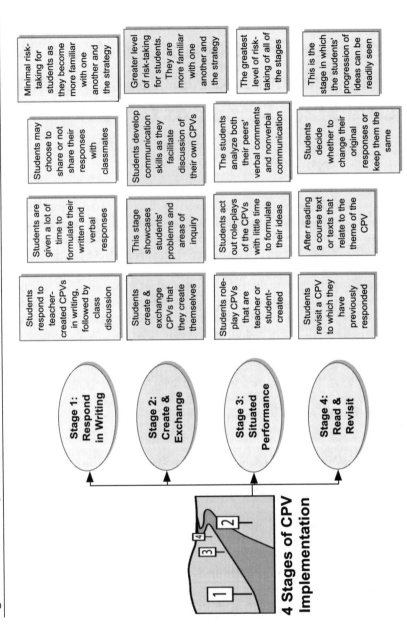

Stage 1: Respond in Writing	Students respond to teacher-created CPVs in writing, followed by class discussion	Students are given a lot of time to formulate their written and verbal responses	Students may choose to share or not share their responses with classmates	Minimal risk-taking for students as they become more familiar with one another and the strategy
Stage 2: Create & Exchange	Students create & exchange CPVs that they create themselves	This stage showcases students' problems and areas of inquiry	Students develop communication skills as they facilitate discussion of their own CPVs	Greater level of risk-taking for students. They are more familiar with one another and the strategy
Stage 3: Situated Performance	Students role-play CPVs that are teacher or student-created	Students act out role-plays of the CPVs with little time to formulate their ideas	The students analyze both their peers' verbal comments and nonverbal communication	The greatest level of risk-taking of all of the stages
Stage 4: Read & Revisit	Students revisit a CPV to which they have previously responded	After reading a course text or texts that relate to the theme of the CPV	Students decide whether to change their original responses or keep them the same	This is the stage in which the students' progression of ideas can be readily seen

4 Stages of CPV Implementation

1
2
3
4

14

at the start of the school year, so it might be helpful to do some ice breakers and team-building activities with students prior to engaging in Stage 1.

It is helpful to assign the first few written CPVs as homework; this allows students to take them home and consider their responses quietly and carefully, without the distractions of the classroom. It is also recommended that in the beginning, teachers ask students to voluntarily share their responses or only aspects of their responses they feel comfortable disclosing. This is a better way to create a safe environment for dialogue about sensitive issues than forcing all students to be spotlighted and share their responses. Another way to help increase students' comfort levels is to have them first share their CPV responses with partners or small groups rather than the entire class.

Students begin by responding to CPVs in writing because they need time to formulate their ideas and are afforded the luxury of deciding which aspects of their responses they want to share with the class. They need time to become comfortable as a group sharing their thoughts and ideas concerning topics that may be rarely addressed. They also need time to gain trust in the teacher as a facilitator of culturally and politically sensitive discussions and to see if and how the teacher creates a class environment of thoughtful sharing and mutual respect.

Stage 2 is the Create and Exchange stage in which students create their own CPVs based on a common theme provided by the teacher (e.g., bullying, racism, nationalism) or based on content-related or behavioral issues with which they might be personally grappling in their classrooms, schools, homes, or communities. The teacher provides students with guidelines for how to create good CPVs, and students are free to develop their own CPV scenarios. The student-created CPVs are then exchanged with peers and can be responded to using a variety of methods. This stage of implementation is a logical follow-up to Stage 1 because it prioritizes students' problems and areas of inquiry over the teacher's. Stage 2 can only be implemented, however, after Stage 1 because students need a good understanding of what CPVs are and models of appropriate responses to CPVs before they have the ability to create and exchange their own. Students also need practice discussing teacher-made CPVs so they can develop the communication skills needed to facilitate their own discussions of student-created CPVs.

When students are writing and responding to their own CPVs and those of their classmates, they are asked to take slightly more risk in the sense that the culturally and politically sensitive issues that they are grappling with in their own lives drive the curriculum; by their very design, student-constructed CPVs are windows into personal issues for which they might be having difficulty finding appropriate solutions. One way to minimize this risk is by making the CPVs anonymous when they are exchanged with others. Either way, however, student-created and exchanged CPVs pose greater risk to students than responding to teacher-made CPVs because they often show the vulnerability of the student who is struggling to find a solution to a personal problem.

The third stage of CPV implementation is often most effectively used later in the school year, once students are comfortable with one another and the teacher and are familiar and comfortable with CPVs as a pedagogical process. During this Situated Performance stage, students act out situated performance role-plays of the CPVs, making the CPV responses far more analogous to what takes place in real life when a politically or culturally sensitive issue or problem occurs with another person or people. Rarely in life is anyone afforded the opportunity to go home and think about a situation and/or write a carefully thought-out response to it prior to confronting the situation at hand and taking action. Accordingly, this stage requires students to respond to the CPVs in near real time, the way they would need to do if the situations actually occurred.

Obviously, this third stage is far more difficult for students than previous stages because it involves honing both verbal and nonverbal communication skills in ways that are likely to be quite foreign to them. The situated performances enable students in the audience several advantages, including viewing their peers and analyzing their verbal comments. In addition, students can discuss nonverbal aspects of CPV performances, such as body language, tones of voice employed, voice volume and pitch, degree of eye contact, and wait time for responses to questions.

Finally, Stage 4 is the Read and Revisit stage of CPV implementation, in which students revisit a CPV to which they have previously responded verbally, in writing, or in the form of a situated performance after reading a course text or texts on a related theme or topic. They then decide if, after having read the text, they would change their original responses to the CPV or keep them the same. Regardless of their decisions, they must provide textual evidence and sound text-based rationales for why they would or would not respond to the CPV differently based on their newly acquired knowledge gleaned from the text.

This stage, like Stage 3, is best implemented after students have engaged in the three previous stages and are comfortable both with CPVs as a pedagogical process and with discussing difficult topics with their classmates and teacher. As is true of Stage 3, Stage 4 is most effective later in the school year, when students are comfortable not only with sharing their responses but also with identifying and articulating changes that they might make to original responses as a direct result of having read a course text or texts. The Read and Revisit stage allows teachers to understand and evaluate respondents' progression of ideas. The teacher can look at students' original responses to a CPV and contrast them with their revisited responses that take place after interacting with course texts and discussion. In this sense, CPVs can serve as both formative and summative assessment tools. Elements that surface during all four stages of CPVs include discussion of one's possible motives for responding in particular ways and the influence of one's personal history on one's decisionmaking within a role enactment.

BULLYING: AN EXAMPLE OF A TEACHER
WORKING THROUGH THE FOUR STAGES

A central theme that is of importance to secondary students and teachers, bullying, was used by a 7th-grade language arts teacher to create CPV activities employing all four stages of CPV implementation over the course of a school year. The teacher decided to use bullying as a year-long CPV theme because she and her colleagues had previously developed an anonymous survey to assess bullying at their school. The results of this survey revealed to the faculty that adults were gravely underestimating the rates and severity of bullying at the school, and that the majority of students believed that teachers were not taking active roles in preventing bullying from occurring or dealing with it effectively when it was brought to their attention. The teacher actively and thoughtfully tailored the bullying CPV activities to meet the needs of her students, in the hope that it would educate and sensitize them to issues surrounding bullying and positively influence their behavior.

The first stage of CPV implementation, which is discussed in greater detail in Chapter 2, involves asking students to respond to teacher-created CPVs and to share their verbal and written responses in pairs and small groups and through whole-class discussion. In the beginning of the school year, the teacher presented the following CPV prompt to her students and asked them to respond in writing for homework:

Imagine that a group of kids at school decide for no reason that they don't like you. They leave nasty notes on your locker, call you bad names at recess, and push you in the hallway and on your way to the bus. What would you do?

When the teacher gave this CPV prompt to her students at the beginning of the school year, she was surprised by how few of them were willing to share their responses aloud the next day with their classmates. She was further surprised at the hopelessness expressed in her students' responses. The majority believed there was nothing they could do to correct the bullying situation and that telling their parents or the teachers would only make the situation worse. The few students in the class who believed they could do something gave avoidance responses such as, "I would try and convince my parents to send me to another school," "I would pretend to be sick and stay home from school for a while and hope that by the time I came back, the teasing would stop," and "I would hide from the kids and ask my mom to pick me up so I wouldn't have to ride the bus."

The teacher asked for student volunteers to share their responses with the whole class, but on getting no volunteers, she chose to read several of the students' anonymous responses aloud to the class herself. Although students were still reticent to react to their classmates' responses, they eventually began to discuss the topic of bullying and to respond to and critique the anonymous responses that the teacher shared. The teacher was relieved when one particularly vocal student commented, "This is really wrong. No one should have to stay home, hide, or go to another school because people are mean to them for no reason." The teacher learned through her students' responses that the theme of bullying was obviously a controversial and important one to address with her students, so she began to devise ways to continue addressing this topic using the four stages of CPV implementation.

The teacher continued to provide her students with age- and developmentally appropriate CPV prompts to respond to in writing for the first few months of the school year. She chose topics that were relevant to her 7th-grade students, often using situations that transpired in class as springboards for her writing prompts. When a new student entered the class a month after school had started, she used a CPV about being new to a school and making friends. When two students got into a physical altercation over a computer in the room, she created a behavioral CPV about sharing resources and taking turns. She did this to familiarize her students with the CPV strategy, as well as to give them the opportunity to get to know one another and feel more comfortable sharing their ideas.

During class discussions that followed students' written responses to CPVs, the teacher made a concerted effort to facilitate the discussions in ways that highlighted students' multiple perspectives, and whenever students said or did disrespectful things, the teacher reacted promptly to curtail the negative comments and behavior. As a result, student dialogue became richer, as more and more students were willing to share and express their thoughts and opinions. Two months after she introduced the first CPV prompt, during which time she had her students practice responding to CPVs once or twice a week, the teacher decided to revisit the bullying theme as part of Stage 2 of CPV implementation, the Create and Exchange stage, in which students write their own CPV prompts and exchange them with partners or in small groups. She provided the following instructions to students:

For homework, please create a CPV for your classmates that relates to the theme of bullying. Please be sure that the problem you present in your CPV can have more than one solution. Please be prepared to exchange your CPV with other students in our class tomorrow.

Student-created CPVs on bullying included the following:

- There is a girl in your class who is overweight, and all the other girls call her bad names, like fat and ugly. Your mom is really overweight and told you how when she was a girl, people made fun of her, and it really hurt her feelings. You love your mom and even though she is big, you think she is a really smart, nice person. What do you do?
- Every day when you get on the bus, an older, bigger boy picks on you and won't let you sit in the seat that you want to sit in. He makes you go to the back of the bus and sit near kids that you don't like. What do you do?
- A girl in your class used to always call you bad names. You are having a birthday party soon, and you notice that the girl has been acting really nice to you all of a sudden. You know that she has heard about your party, and you think that she wants to come. What do you do?
- You are getting bullied really badly at school, and the principal calls you in to the office to talk about it. He wants to call the parents of the kids who are doing it, but he wants your permission first. What do you do?

The teacher chose to have students share their CPVs in groups of four, and she asked group members to respond to their peers' CPVs initially in writing. She also asked the student who created the CPV to act as discussion leader when students shared and discussed their responses verbally. She remarked that although it was difficult at times for her to give students so much power and control during the activity, she believed that the dialogue that they had surrounding their own CPVs was decidedly richer than the one they had in response to her bullying CPV in September. She attributed this success both to students' increased familiarity with the strategy and one another and to the fact that the students' own problem posing was now helping to shape the curriculum.

To further explore the bullying CPVs that her students had previously created and exchanged, the 7th-grade language arts teacher chose to implement the third stage of CPV implementation, Situated Performance, in the middle of the school year. She chose three of the student-created bullying CPVs as prompts for the student role-plays and assigned the same prompt to two groups, so that students viewing the performances would have the opportunity to compare and contrast two different responses to each CPV. One of the CPVs the teacher chose for students to perform was this one:

A new kid comes into your school and class from another town, and he is already being made fun of by the kids. The teacher makes you be his partner in class and asks you to sit next to him and help him. Your best friend threatens to stop hanging out with you because this new kid follows you around in school. What do you do?

In response to this CPV, two groups created situated performances. The first group chose to have the student who was paired with the new kid confront his best friend when he threatens to stop hanging out with him, whereas the second group chose to have the student who was paired with the new kid confront the new kid and ask him to please stop following him around outside of class. The students in the audience evaluated both situated performances critically, and most believed that the first group had presented a more socially just solution. Other students disagreed and argued that in the real world, the second group's response, although not as "nice," was more realistic and authentic in terms of what would happen. The students critically evaluated not only the responses to the CPV depicted in situated performances, but also the gestures, posture, intonation, and various other non-verbal characteristics of the student actors. They became more adept at critiquing the CPV responses as a result of seeing them "unfold" before their eyes in class.

Near the conclusion of the school year, in the spring, the teacher chose to implement the fourth and final stage of CPV implementation, Read and Revisit. She did this after her students had read and written about several texts that contain the theme of bullying, including Gordon Korman's *Schooled* (2007), Jerry Spinelli's *Stargirl* (2000), and Walter Dean Myers's *Shooter* (2005). The students also attended a schoolwide assembly in April, during which guest speakers from a local adolescent mental health agency talked about the dangers of bullying and presented students with both local and online resources to help stop bullying in their school and community.

As part of the Read and Revisit activities, the teacher asked students to revisit the original bullying CPV to which they had responded back in September. The teacher had collected and kept the student responses to this CPV in a folder and returned them to her students with the following directions:

Please read your response to a CPV that you wrote back in September about bullying. After having read several books about this topic and attending the assembly, would you still respond to this CPV in the same way today? Why or why not? Please explain and use at least three references from the texts and/or the assembly to explain why you would change your earlier response or keep it the same.

Most students in this 7th-grade class were surprised to read what they had written in response to this CPV just 8 months earlier. Many were displeased by how apathetic their original responses were and were eager to discuss the changes in their thinking over time and exposure to the new knowledge they had acquired from the texts and assembly. One student summed up these changes in her thinking by writing the following:

I am really embarrassed about what I wrote back in September. I realize now that bullying is a very serious thing and that kids have actually killed themselves and others as a result of bullying. I realize now how wrong it is and have zero tolerance for bullies around me, my brothers and sisters, and my friends. I hope that if more kids become aware like I have, we can save lives in the future.

GUIDELINES FOR CREATING CPVS

You and your high school students can use the following guidelines to create effective, thought-provoking CPVs. They may be reworded using less complex language for younger students or others who would benefit from simplified directions:

- Be sure that the CPV is open-ended and does not have one or even two obvious, clear-cut correct responses. The topic of the CPV should be sufficiently complex to stimulate reflection on the part of the people responding to it and should encourage them to consider several cultural and/or political factors when responding. There should be several appropriate responses to a CPV and sound rationales for why these responses to the CPV would be reasonable.
- Use language that is appropriate for the respondents for whom the CPV is intended. Don't overcomplicate the CPV with language that is too difficult

or might dissuade or prevent respondents from understanding the central problem or situation being presented in the CPV. Keep it simple!

- Try to make the CPV as realistic as possible. This is often accomplished by reflecting on your own life experiences or those of others, including people you know, fictional literary characters, or people you encounter through media.
- A thought-provoking CPV will compel respondents to consider aspects of culture and/or politics with which they might not be completely familiar or comfortable. This is an integral part of CPVs and should be encouraged.
- If a CPV is well constructed, it will stimulate debate, discussion, and perhaps even anger on the part of respondents. Those responding to the CPV might come away feeling frustrated or confused, but this is a fundamental part of the CPV process—a direct and anticipated result of asking them to consider complex issues in ways to which they might not be accustomed.

The preceding guidelines are not set in stone, and as you become more adept at working with CPVs, there are endless ways to adapt them to students, course texts, outcome expectations, and so on. The most important thing to remember is that CPVs are invitations for respondents to explore a problem or issue from multiple perspectives; in order for them to do so, the CPV prompt must be designed to promote critical analysis and reflection.

TAILORING CONTENT AND PRESENTATION OF CPVS TO DIFFERENT LEVELS

There are several ways in which you can tailor the content, presentation, and academic tasks that accompany CPVs to different age and ability levels. CPVs for middle school students will typically be less complex than for high school students. For example, a middle school CPV on substance abuse might read as follows:

One of your friends has been stealing beer and cigarettes from his mom and using them after school. At first, you weren't concerned about it, but lately you notice that he has started smoking every day before and after school and drinking beer every weekend. You don't want your friend to get into trouble with teachers or his parents, but you are afraid that he might be becoming addicted. You notice that he has become very quiet in school, doesn't want to play sports any more, and failed his last math test. What do you do?

At the middle school level, students are capable of analyzing this CPV in depth and looking at it through several lenses. In this CPV, there may be an element of activation of prior knowledge, as students might be able to draw from their own life experiences when thinking about the details of a substance abuse situation. Middle school students can also make text-to-self, text-to-world, and text-to-text connections to a CPV on substance abuse because of things they have encountered in their own lives, on television, in films, online, and through books and other texts. This CPV touches on issues surrounding peer pressure, the question of whether to betray a friend's trust when he or she might be in physical or emotional danger, and the warning signs that a teenager might be experimenting with or abusing drugs and/or alcohol.

In thinking about the potential literacy tasks associated with this CPV, you might ask students to respond in writing initially, have a class discussion, and later use this CPV as part of a Read and Revisit activity. You might ask students to respond in writing, read several texts (both fiction and nonfiction) that deal with the theme of substance abuse, and perhaps invite a guest speaker to discuss possible actions that students can take when engaging in or witnessing substance abuse. Later, you could ask students to revisit their original written responses and assess how they might integrate their newly acquired knowledge about substance abuse into an improved response to the CPV. An appropriate culminating literacy task at the middle school level might be to ask students to write narrative essays explaining the changes to their CPV responses after reading the substance abuse texts and hearing the guest speaker, using evidence from the texts and speaker's presentation to support their changes.

At the high school level, in grades 9 through 12, a substance abuse CPV could be expanded on and further complicated to involve prescription drug abuse, a serious problem facing adults and secondary school students today. In recent years there have been violent robberies involving the theft of prescription drugs from pharmacies in the United States, and this topic is receiving increasing media attention. A high school CPV on prescription substance abuse might read as follows:

Six months ago, your mother was in a car accident and badly injured her back. As a result, the doctor prescribed her a drug called Oxycodone to alleviate her pain. As time has passed, you are noticing serious changes in your mom's behavior. She has no appetite, sleeps all the time, and does not enjoy doing activities that she used to enjoy. When her Oxycodone prescription ran out, she went to a second doctor, who prescribed her another painkiller called Vicodin. You know that your mother's back pain is serious, but you believe that she has become addicted to the pills that the doctors are prescribing. What do you do?

As with the preceding example for middle school, this more complex substance abuse CPV could also be responded to in writing, discussed verbally, and then revisited after reading class texts and listening to a guest speaker. The topic itself is far more complex than the middle school example because the drugs in this example are prescribed by doctors rather than being obtained illegally and consumed by an underaged person. A debate would surely arise about when people should seek additional opinions in medical situations. Also, you could incorporate related issues from the popular media and current events into the CPV activities, such as violent pharmacy robberies and the release of Michael Jackson's doctor, Conrad Murray, from prison, after serving 2 years (of a 4-year sentence) for his medical involvement in Jackson's wrongful death. This CPV is also far more complex because the child in the CPV is witnessing substance abuse in his or her *parent*, rather than in a peer. This would significantly affect the complexity of the situation and how high school students might approach this CPV topic from multiple perspectives.

There are many follow-up literacy activities that could be generated by the high school students themselves with regard to this CPV, or you could ask students to do one or more of the following tasks: Create brochures on prescription drug abuse prevention to distribute to other students, parents, teachers, and administrators at the school; invite a specially trained social worker or medical expert to talk to the class or school about prescription drug addiction prevention techniques; speak to younger students (at the middle school level) about prescription drug abuse and its consequences and prevention; or create an informational presentation for parents in the community about prescription drug abuse awareness.

One recommendation for presenting CPVs to middle school students is the use of modeling through the fishbowl method (Eitington, 1996). In this method, four to five chairs are arranged in an inner circle—the fishbowl. Remaining chairs are arranged in concentric circles outside the fishbowl. A few participants are selected to fill the fishbowl, and remaining group members sit on the chairs outside the fishbowl. In an open fishbowl, one chair is always left empty. In a closed fishbowl, all chairs are filled. The moderator introduces the topic, and participants start discussion. The audience outside of the fishbowl listens in on the discussion and benefits from the modeling.

It is helpful to select several students with strong communication skills to model aspects of CPV activities for their classmates. The fishbowl can be used to model an effective group discussion of a CPV prompt and/or a CPV situated performance. Through watching their peers in the fishbowl, middle school students gain confidence in their own abilities to successfully engage in CPV activities and gain helpful perspectives on what these activities look like when done appropriately.

Conversely, when presenting CPVs to high school students, you might choose to model and employ more advanced discussion techniques with which students may or may not be familiar, such as Socratic circles or seminars (Copeland, 2010; Mangrum, 2010). These methods, named after the Greek philosopher Socrates, are forms of inquiry and discussion among individuals, based on asking and answering questions to stimulate critical thinking and illuminate ideas. The methods are dialectical, typically involving a discussion in which the defense of one point of view is questioned, and one participant might lead another to contradict him- or herself in some way, thus strengthening the inquirer's own point.

Socratic circles or seminars work well with discussions that begin with CPV prompts because CPV problems can always be viewed through multiple lenses and promote thoughtful and respectful dialogue. The two pedagogical approaches—Socratic circles or seminars and CPVs—have many similarities in that both involve problem posing and problem solving; critical dialogue; an emphasis on listening to others' ideas and subsequently altering your own; and questioning speakers' motives, personal histories, cultural and political biases, prior knowledge and experiences, and other factors that contribute to a person's point of view on a controversial topic.

HOW TO AVOID COMMON CPV PITFALLS
AND STRENGTHEN CPV PROMPTS

One of the most common issues that teachers and secondary students have in creating CPVs involves presenting a problem that does not have one clear-cut, obvious, or correct answer. For example, the following CPV was originally written by a high school Participation in Government teacher for use with her 12th-grade students:

You lost a family member when terrorists attacked the World Trade Center on September 11, 2001. Your family is very upset to learn that a mosque will be built a block away from Ground Zero. What do you do?

As you can see from the wording of this CPV, it leads the respondent in one particular direction and does not allow students to explore multiple perspectives or viewpoints in response. The teacher who created the CPV revised it to read:

You lost a family member when terrorists attacked the World Trade Center on September 11, 2001. You just received a survey in the mail from a group of NYC landowners that reads: A mosque might be built a block away from Ground Zero next year, and we want to take your opinion into consideration before construction begins. Do you approve or object? Why?

The teacher also added the following stipulation: "Please account for the following in your response: How is this issue related to the First Amendment right to Freedom of Religion?" By changing the wording of the CPV to make it more objective and asking respondents to consider the First Amendment, the teacher created a more complex CPV that invites several interpretations and encourages respondents to consider the CPV through multiple lenses.

Another common mistake that teachers make with regard to writing CPVs is making them too complex or so tailored to a particular text that they become inauthentic. For example, an 8th-grade language arts teacher created the following CPV for use with Shirley Jackson's short story "The Lottery":

You have just moved into a new, small town. You don't know anyone, and really want to make friends. A group of kids approach you and ask you to hang out with them. Being a new kid, you jump at the opportunity. Afterward, however, you realize they are not so great. They do things you don't feel comfortable with (hurt others and act violently). However, nobody else in town seems to mind (adults and children), and in fact sometimes join in. Do you continue to follow the crowd in order to avoid standing out? What are the consequences of saying no? What would you do in this situation?

This CPV, in its current form, is so aligned with "The Lottery," a work of fiction, that it becomes less authentic and a bit forced. The teacher created a more realistic version of this CPV by removing a few details:

You have just moved into a new town. You don't know anyone, and want to make friends. A group of kids approach you and ask you to hang out with them. Being a new kid, you jump at the opportunity. After a short time, however, you realize they do things you don't feel comfortable with (hurt others and act violently). What would you do in this particular situation?

By streamlining the wording of the CPV and removing the parts that directly referenced "The Lottery," the teacher made the CPV more realistic. It is still aligned with the theme of "The Lottery" and the issue of complacency in the face of violence, but it no longer leads the respondent down an unrealistic path. Word choice in the creation of CPVs is very important. Sometimes changing even a word or two can significantly affect the way a person views the problem being posed and his or her subsequent response. Figure 1.2 provides several suggestions for avoiding common pitfalls and strengthening CPV prompts.

Figure 1.2. Avoiding Common Pitfalls and Strengthening CPV Prompts

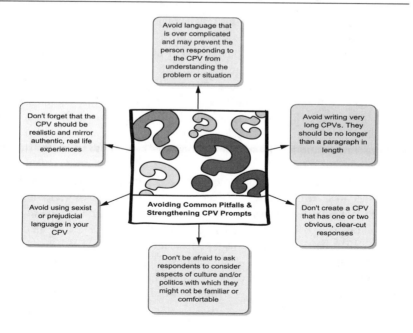

Similarly, you might need to work with your secondary students to improve CPVs during the second stage of CPV Implementation—the Create and Exchange stage—in which students write their own CPVs and exchange them with classmates. In addition to the aforementioned issues concerning the complexity of the situation and its authenticity, students might need help with avoiding sexist or prejudicial language in their CPVs; using language that is overcomplicated or confusing to respondents; writing CPVs that are too long; or being afraid to ask respondents to consider aspects of culture and politics with which they might not be familiar or comfortable. The best way to ensure that you and your students can write good CPV prompts and strengthen weaker ones is by providing many models for them prior to asking them to create CPVs themselves. This need for modeling is one of several reasons why Stage 1 of CPV implementation involves responding in writing to CPVs that have been written by others.

CPVS AS A MEANS OF DIFFERENTIATING INSTRUCTION

CPVs enable you to more easily differentiate instruction because they are malleable and can be easily broken down into smaller learning objectives. At a time when we are facing increased diversity among students in our classrooms, it is progressively more helpful to have pedagogical tools at our disposal that help make the differentiation of instruction more seamless and viable. Although school administrators value and look for differentiation of instruction when observing and supervising teachers, they rarely provide professional training or suggestions for how differentiation can be accomplished. CPVs can help us to fill this pedagogical void. CPVs can also aid us in making available safe spaces for students of all ability levels to engage in meaningful, respectful dialogue about culturally and politically complex and sensitive issues.

In terms of presentation, middle school or high school students who require greater academic support in their instruction, such as special education students and ELLs, require greater scaffolding and more modeling of CPV activities than do their peers. They require more explicit directions with regard to how to respond to CPVs, discuss them, create their own, create role-plays, critique one another's responses, and so forth. As a result, it can be helpful to provide academic support teachers, such as resource room and ESL teachers, with copies of the CPVs to which the students will be responding prior to the due date. This way, students can practice writing and sharing their responses in smaller, more supportive learning environments before being asked to share their CPVs in larger mainstreamed classrooms. This is a common practice with students who receive academic support services, and this extra time and practice go a long way toward contributing to their successes on difficult academic tasks, particularly those with performance elements.

For students who have writing disabilities and require accommodations, such as scribes or the use of laptop computers to write, CPV responses can be given verbally to a teacher first and later written or word processed. The key to ensuring that special-needs students will be successful on CPV activities is to break the activities down and provide students with the additional time, academic support, and scaffolding that they need. These modifications are not intended to create extra work for teachers and students, but rather to help them interact with controversial material in ways that are more engaging, exploratory, and participatory. CPVs can also be easily modified and broken into smaller components to help suit the diverse learning needs and abilities of special education students and English language learners.

In a high school English class, for example, you might choose to group students by ability levels and give a middle school–level CPV to students with learning disabilities or serious language barriers, rather than a more complex, high school–level CPV. This way, students in need of differentiation or additional support respond to a modified CPV that addresses the same central theme being considered by the rest of the students. Ideally, the English or social studies teacher would work in conjunction with a special educator, such as a resource room teacher or an ESL or bilingual support staff member, and give the less complex CPV to that support teacher, so that he or she can work on it with the student prior to the date when it would be presented and discussed in English or social studies class.

A resource room special education teacher can frontload the learning experience by giving the special-needs student opportunities to gain prior knowledge and have extra time to consider and respond to the CPV. The CPV might be discussed in resource room first and then an extra step or two, such as asking the student to complete an outline, graphic organizer, or some other prewriting activity, might be added to the process to scaffold the activity and make it more feasible. In the case of situated performances, special-needs students might be given a chance to rehearse their skits in the resource room prior to being asked to perform them in front of the English or social studies class, thus reducing their stage fright and making them more willing and able to fully participate. In providing CPVs to the support staff so they can practice aspects of the CPV activities with special-needs students, you are successfully differentiating instruction while still holding special-needs students to high standards and asking all students to dialogue and problem-solve around the central theme of bullying.

For English language learners (ELLs), an alternative might be to simply reword the CPV using more simple language or to translate the CPV into their native languages and allow them to respond in their home languages on their first drafts. Afterward, they could be given support in translating their responses into English and sharing them with the class. Obviously, when teaching ELLs, particularly those who are in the emerging stages of their English language literacy development and are struggling readers and writers of English, all aspects of the four CPV stages might not be fully utilized, and all of the CPV prompts and responses might not be presented to students in writing. For these students, you can elicit responses verbally and may also ask them to respond in writing in the form of brainstorming and writing lists of words, writing one-sentence responses, filling in graphic organizers, or even drawing pictures.

ELLs, particularly from certain countries, might be entirely uncomfortable expressing their personal opinions, especially with regard to controversial or sensitive issues that deal with race, gender, religion, or culture. In their native countries, they may never have been exposed to pedagogical strategies that rely heavily on self-expression of opinions, and they might require additional assistance in understanding the American teachers' expectations. They might find it strange that you are eliciting their opinions and might first need practice talking and writing about what they think and feel, which they may never have done in their previous schooling abroad. When working with ELLS on CPVs, it might be helpful for them to use writing prompts such as "I think . . . ," "I feel . . . ," and "I believe . . ." in order to practice self-expression prior to responding to CPVs directly in writing.

IMPORTANCE OF CLASSROOM CULTURE AND THE TEACHER'S ROLE

Figure 1.3 depicts "how to" tips for creating a positive classroom climate for CPVs. The single most important factor in determining whether students will become comfortable expressing their thoughts and sharing their responses involves the classroom climate or culture that you create during class discussions of CPVs. It is critical that you model open-minded, respectful dialogue among students so they feel their voices are heard and that their opinions are truly desired and respected by you and their peers. Without a climate of mutual respect in the class, it is impossible to ask students to share their ideas about such controversial issues as race, gender, politics, religion, culture, homosexuality, and bullying.

When a student shares a response to a CPV that you believe is potentially offensive, upsetting, or off-putting to other students, you must intervene immediately, and in such a way that you are not shutting down the offending student or others in the class. One way to do this is to say something like, "Although some of you might disagree with Annie's point of view, we are looking at this situation from multiple perspectives, and Annie has a right to her opinion. In this class, even if we disagree with one another at times, we are here to learn from each other's perspectives and can agree to disagree."

There are times, of course, when student opinions are so offensive (or potentially offensive) that you *must* discourage students from voicing them. The best way to decide where to draw the line is by asking yourself if the opinion being voiced is offensive enough that it could hurt students in the class, incite potential violence, or oppress other students to the extent that they will no longer be willing to engage in discussions with the offending student and others. Typically, comments that are racist, sexist, or homophobic must be stopped immediately. Boundaries must be clearly communicated to students to prevent problems and disruption during class discussions.

One strategy for establishing boundaries is to tell students they should speak as if their grandparents and classmates' grandparents are listening to them.

Figure 1.3. "How to" Tips for Creating a Positive Classroom Climate for CPVs

When a student shares a response to a CPV that the teacher believes may be potentially offensive, upsetting or off-putting to other students, she must intervene immediately and do so in such a way that she is not shutting down the offending student or the others in the class

The teacher also needs to be able to put her own personal views to the side and not bring significant biases to the table

The discussions around CPV issues can get quite heated, so it is necessary that the teacher take a very active role in facilitating a respectful, balanced discussion

Although she may disagree with her students' views on these controversial issues, it is important that she try not to force her viewpoints on to the students in any way

"How to" Tips for Creating a Positive Classroom Climate for CPVs

It is critical that the teacher model open-minded, respectful dialogue among the students

If students feel disrespected or are mocked by their peers when sharing their responses, then the whole process breaks down and students will be unwilling to participate

Another is to suggest they should not say anything they wouldn't want their parents or the principal of the school to hear. One high school teacher that I observed told his students that they should speak to one another as if they were running for political office and everything they said was going to be televised. Another teacher approached this issue by having her students construct their own Rules for CPV Discussions, in which they outlined what they believed was inappropriate or offensive. Their rules included: no profanity or name-calling, no use of derogatory language toward other students, no calling others' ideas dumb or stupid, and no laughing or interrupting when others are speaking. Secondary students are often quite adept at creating their own rules, and when they are involved in the process, the buy-in is often greater than when the rules are imposed by teachers.

The discussions of CPV issues can get quite heated, so it is necessary that you take a very active role in facilitating a respectful, balanced discussion. If you fail to do so, and if students feel disrespected or are mocked by their peers when sharing their responses, the whole process breaks down. Students will be unwilling to participate, and rightfully so. This will make it impossible to move to the later stages of CPV implementation.

Privacy and confidentiality can also come into play with regard to CPVs and your role. When students create and exchange their own CPVs, or when you share students' individual responses to CPVs with the whole class, you might decide that it is in the best interest of the students to maintain their privacy and confidentiality. This is principally important when students are using CPVs as platforms for dealing with personal problems or issues that they do not want revealed to their classmates. You can handle this situation in several ways, ranging from having students submit CPVs anonymously to having them put a letter P for private on the top right corner if they do not want their CPV or response shared. Other ways to address privacy and confidentiality issues include having students only share voluntarily or only share those aspects of their CPVs and responses with which they feel comfortable. For CPV activities to be successful, students have to trust that you and their fellow classmates are going to respect their privacy and maintain their confidentiality when requested.

You also need to be able to put your own personal views to the side and try not to bring significant biases to the table. An example of this could be a religious teacher who has certain views about homosexuality, same-sex marriage, infidelity, or premarital sex that are dictated by her religious beliefs and affiliation. Although she may disagree with some of her students' views on these controversial issues, it is important that she avoid sharing her opinions, thus potentially influencing her students via her authoritative position in the classroom (Darvin, 2011a). Similarly, students with particular religious views should not be allowed to inflict their religious beliefs on classmates or use religion as a way to judge, embarrass, or preach to others.

At the same time, students with strict religious views should not be made to feel they are being ridiculed or judged because their views on social issues are in the minority. The religion issue is analogous to a history teacher who is teaching a unit to secondary students on an upcoming presidential election. The teacher is supposed to explore and discuss the political process with his students, not try to influence them to support a particular candidate with whom he might be politically aligned.

In closing, you must make concerted efforts to remain judgment free and keep your biases and those of your students from negatively influencing CPV discussions. This does not mean shutting people's opinions down, but does require framing them in ways that demonstrate to all that everyone has a right to his or her particular viewpoint. This will help students understand that the CPV prompts are intentionally open-ended and do not have right or wrong answers. It will also add to a climate of trust and mutual respect among class members.

THE NEED FOR COLLABORATION WITH OTHERS
AND OBTAINING PARENTAL PERMISSIONS

In order to create a climate of trust and respect that extends beyond the students in the classroom and into the school and larger community, you might need to collaborate with both parents and other school personnel to ensure the success of certain CPV activities. Some of the additional personnel with whom you may choose to collaborate include literacy coaches, reading specialists, ESL teachers, special educators, and others who provide academic support services to students. These collaborations can help with both the planning and execution of CPV activities and can provide students with the appropriate scaffolding, modeling, and additional academic resources they might need to be successful with CPV units.

Additionally, there might be times when it is appropriate for you to reach out to your department chair, assistant principal, principal, or an administrator who deals with curriculum and instruction in your school or district to let him or her know about the CPV unit and its controversial subject matter. Administrators should also be alerted whenever you are planning to invite guests from the community to come speak to your students or you are planning any schoolwide initiatives or CPV activities that might extend beyond your classroom walls and into the larger school or community contexts.

There might also be times when it is necessary and prudent to collaborate with school guidance counselors, psychologists, or other mental health professionals in your school to help you deal with content that might be upsetting or disturbing to some students. Typically, when discussing very serious and controversial issues such as suicide, genocide, euthanasia, and other dark topics, it is recommended to collaborate with school personnel who are trained to deal with students' emotional reactions and psychological health. It is not recommended that you broach tough issues such as these in the classroom by yourself. It is best to have a support system in place for students as you plan controversial and potentially upsetting CPV units, and know going into them that some students might need the support of counselors to deal with these difficult topics.

On other occasions, it might be wise to collaborate with community members and resources whose expertise goes beyond that of school personnel. School psychologists and counselors might believe that it is necessary to invite outside experts on particular issues, such as drug abuse, suicide, or mental illness, to come and speak to your students as part of the CPV unit. These community members might be more skilled at discussing these highly controversial and upsetting topics than are school personnel, and also might be able to make resources available to students that school personnel cannot.

The determination whether or not a community resource should be invited into the classroom is a decision best made jointly between you, the classroom teacher, an administrator, and possibly a school counselor or psychologist. There are countless community organizations that are willing and able to give highly informative presentations in secondary schools and that welcome the opportunity to do so. The school counselors are a good starting place for you to locate such resources. Additionally, local police departments, mental health agencies, drug and alcohol counseling centers, and community centers are good places to begin looking for guest speakers who are appropriate to speak with secondary students as part of CPV units.

Along these same lines, it is extremely important that parents are notified when you will be reading texts, showing films, inviting guest speakers, and writing about and discussing highly complex and controversial topics as part of CPV units. To determine whether parental permission is required, you should discuss your plans for your CPV unit with your departmental chair or the assistant principal to see if they believe that the content is sensitive enough to require parental consent.

Parental permission letters should describe the nature of the controversial material that will be presented to students and include a detailed rationale for how and why you are choosing to discuss this controversial topic with your secondary students. In my experience, it is helpful if the CPV unit can also be discussed with parents at a PTA meeting, open-school night, or other school forum. It is preferable to talk to parents about your plans in addition to writing about them because it gives parents the opportunity to ask questions and better understand your curricular goals and objectives.

It is also important that you create parallel assignments for those students whose parents decide they do not want their children present and/or do not want them exposed to certain concepts and discussions in school. These makeup assignments must contain significant rigor and be equivalent to the work that the students are missing as a result of being unable to participate in the CPV unit.

HOW CPVS HELP TEACHERS REALIZE THE CCSS AND DEVELOP CAPACITIES OF LITERATE INDIVIDUALS

Most states have adopted the 2010 Common Core State Standards (CCSS) for use in the K–12 public schools, and most of the curricular goals of the CCSS are likely to be shared across any program that aims to help students become college and/or career ready. Most state and professional organizations' standards for reading, writing, speaking, and listening effectively, including those established by the National Council of Teachers of English (NCTE), the International Reading Association (IRA), and the National Council for the Social Studies (NCSS) overlap with the CCSS and have many of the same requirements for secondary students.

Although the CCSS outline in great detail what students should be able to understand and do by the end of each grade, they purposefully contain little information about *how* teachers are supposed to ensure that highly complex forms of learning occur in their classrooms. It is the intention of the CCSS to leave room for individual teachers and states to determine how curricular goals should be met in classrooms rather than to mandate particular programs, strategies, or teaching processes.

This focus on results rather than means leaves room for teachers to explore many curricular options, but it also leaves many teachers and school administrators to determine how to achieve the complex and highly specific goals set forth in the standards. This book complements the CCSS by focusing on teaching strategies, as well as pedagogical processes with which teachers can help fulfill the CCSS and other state and national mandates in their classrooms, while concomitantly helping to develop in their students the literacy and language capacities that will ensure they are college and career ready.

One important aspect of the CCSS is that they advocate an *integrated* model of literacy, one in which reading, writing, speaking, listening, and language are closely connected and integrated as communication processes in teaching and learning. The pedagogical strategies depicted in this volume will help you to understand and create such a unified literacy model in your classroom by requiring students to effectively use all five of the CCSS communication processes in meaningful and interconnected ways. Specifics on exactly how this unified literacy model is fostered by the teaching strategies and processes depicted in this book are provided in subsequent chapters.

Additionally, the CCSS and other state standards affirm that American students, in particular, need greater exposure to reading complex *informational* text independently across a variety of content areas. Teachers, however, need support in how to teach informational texts more effectively and need models of innovative teaching strategies, like CPVs, that can be paired with informational texts. Traditionally, we present informational texts to our students predominantly in the areas of math, science, history, and technology in the form of lectures, PowerPoint presentations, Q & A, and other chalk-and-talk methods that do not foster the kind of exposure that will lead them to the higher-level questioning and thinking skills called for by the CCSS.

This book demonstrates several ways in which you can pair informational texts with CPVs in secondary classes across all subject areas, while requiring of students the kinds of creativity and higher-level problem-posing and problem-solving skills needed to meet the CCSS and ultimately their careers and lives as literate adults.

Maloch and Bomer make several salient points about the teaching of informational texts in their article "Teaching about and with Informational Texts: What Does Research Tell Us?" (2013). This article was part of a two-part *Research and Policy* column aimed at addressing how informational texts are defined and used within the CCSS. The authors assert that informational texts, even more so than narrative or fictional texts, involve more extensive integration of modes of language and literacy, using all available tools of thinking and learning (p. 442). The pedagogical strategies outlined in this book can be used just as effectively with informational texts as with fictional ones.

Maloch and Bomer go on to say that teachers should put a range of informational texts into the hands of students, guide them through authentic activities with those texts, and involve students in active dialogue about those texts (p. 446).

They close their column by asserting that "explicit instruction is only effective for real reading and writing inasmuch as it is situated within authentic opportunities for reading and writing informational texts—opportunities that reflect what children might encounter outside of school" (p. 446). Active dialogue about texts and the authentic, real-world opportunities for reading and writing to which they refer are the very hallmarks of the CPV strategies presented in this book.

Proponents of literacy in the content areas should note that the CCSS call for greater shared responsibility for students' literacy development by all teachers, even those outside of the arenas of literacy, reading, writing, language arts, and English. This book will address how secondary teachers of several disciplines can work more effectively with informational and fictional texts in their classrooms, lending support to teachers who are not normally thought of as being directly responsible for literacy instruction per se, to help them better define and understand the critical roles they, too, can play in students' literacy development across the curricula.

In their portrait of students who are college and career ready, the CCSS advocate that as students advance through the grades and master the CCSS, "they are able to exhibit with increasing fullness and regularity [these] capacities of the literate individual" (National Governors Association Center, 2010, p. 7). These CCSS capacities of the literate individual include a demonstration of independence; building strong content knowledge; responding to the varying demands of audience, task, purpose, and discipline; comprehending as well as critiquing; valuing evidence; using technology and digital media capably; and coming to understand other perspectives and cultures.

This book contains a series of pedagogical strategies that speak to all of the CCSS capacities of the literate individual and can help you and your students to develop them in targeted, scaffolded ways. These aspects of the CCSS speak to lifelong skills that move beyond the limited realms of school and standardized testing and into the broader, more lasting educational spheres of good communication skills and ongoing learning.

The CCSS are trying to accomplish many things in the area of literacy, including a more integrated model of literacy in classrooms, greater shared responsibility for students' literacy development across subject areas and grade levels, a more balanced diet of fictional and informational texts, and the development of capacities of literate individuals, to name a few. The four stages of CPV implementation described in the following chapters are designed to help you achieve the desired outcomes of the CCSS by providing you with guidelines and examples of teaching processes that will help the standards be achieved in your classroom. Grounded in several educational theoretical perspectives—including critical literacy, situated cognition and performance, and narrative inquiry—CPVs are designed to help you address culturally and politically sensitive issues in your classroom while allowing students to engage in meaningful problem posing and problem solving within a safe environment.

CHAPTER 2

Stage 1 of CPV Implementation

Responding to Teacher-Created CPVs in Writing

Stage 1 of CPV implementation involves students responding to behavioral or content-driven teacher-created CPVs in writing and engaging in class discussions about their responses or aspects of their responses that they choose to share with their classmates. It is the CPV stage in which you, the teacher, have the greatest control over the CPV activities and should strive to help your students create a classroom climate that allows them to be successful as they gain greater control over the CPV activities in the next three stages.

CRITICAL LITERACY AND NARRATIVES OF EXPERIENCE PROVIDE THEORETICAL FRAMEWORKS FOR STAGE 1

The first stage of working with CPVs is rooted in the theories surrounding the power of dialogue, problem solving, and critical literacy. Paolo Freire's (1970) groundbreaking book about critical literacy and education, *Pedagogy of the Oppressed,* provides several pillars of the theoretical framework that support this first stage of CPV implementation. These include his concepts of *conscientizacao,* the power of dialogue to name the world and his emphasis on dialogue leading to transformative action. *Conscientizacao* can be translated to mean "critical consciousness." Considering and responding to CPVs raises students' critical consciousness by asking them to consider problems from multiple perspectives and to analyze difficult questions that do not have clear answers.

Stage 1 of implementing CPVs also asks students to reveal, explore, refine, and articulate what Connelly and Clandinin (1988) called their own "narratives of experience." From this theoretical perspective, experience is the primary agency of education (Eisner, 1988) and "the more we understand ourselves and can articulate why we are what we are, do what we do, and are headed where we have chosen, the more meaningful our curriculum will be" (p. 11).

Along similar lines, Connelly and Clandinin (1988) and Clandinin (2013) refer to "personal practical knowledge" as being present in our minds, bodies, and practices and acknowledge that people say and do different things under different circumstances. Conversely, different circumstances bring forward different aspects of people's prior experiences that bear on a situation. These dialectic relationships among personal practical knowledge, narratives of experience, and situational context are evident when students respond to CPVs verbally and in writing because they demonstrate through their responses what the hypothetical situations pull from them practically, emotionally, morally, and aesthetically.

The narratives of experience perspective views teachers as active curriculum makers (Craig & Ross, 2008; Huber, Caine, Huber, & Steeves, 2013) rather than passive implementers of curricula developed by others. This perspective emphasizes the control and agency of teachers in creating curriculum and both recognizes and celebrates the inherent interconnectedness between knowledge, experience, and action. The distinctions between the conflicting images concerning teacher as curriculum maker verses curriculum implementer are central to your initial work with CPVs because one of the major goals of CPV activities is to empower you with regard to your curricular decisionmaking.

Regardless of how or why you create a CPV, however, you are always providing an invitation for your students to construct verbal or written narratives of experience, raise their critical consciousness, and evaluate other points of view critically and constructively, all goals of critical literacy and its adjacent theoretical perspectives.

McLaughlin and DeVoogd (2004) developed four principles of critical literacy that are helpful in understanding what critical literacy is and how it functions. Their four principles state the following:

1. Critical literacy focuses on issues of power and promotes reflection, transformation, and action.
2. Critical literacy focuses on the problem and its complexity.
3. Techniques that promote critical literacy are dynamic and adapt to the contexts in which they are used.
4. Examining multiple perspectives is an important aspect of critical literacy. (pp. 54–55)

These four principles are in direct alignment with students responding to teacher-made CPVs verbally and in writing and help to provide theoretical support for how responding to CPVs bolsters critical literacy development in classrooms. When asking students to react and respond to content-specific situations and problems, either verbally or in writing, students are encouraged to focus on issues of power and examine situations from multiple viewpoints and perspectives. CPVs ask students to use their prior knowledge of content in ways that go deeper than simply answering recall or comprehension questions.

Responding to CPVs verbally and in writing are pedagogical strategies that inherently promote critical literacy because by their very design, as stated in the third of McLaughlin and DeVoogd's principles, they are dynamic and can be adapted to the contexts in which they are used. Additionally, asking students to respond to teacher-made CPVs verbally and in writing promotes both critical literacy and critical thinking because CPVs encourage students to become less reliant on a single print text by asking them to synthesize information from various sources in order to inform their decisionmaking processes and juxtapose texts with conflicting meanings (Morgan, 1997), aspects of critical literacy that are also conveniently and directly aligned to the Common Core State Standards (CCSS). Responding to CPVs verbally and in writing advances students' uses of various texts and varied language experiences (Hansen, 2009) and helps students challenge the information presented in textbooks (Patterson & Speed, 2007). CPVs ask students to interact with content-specific situations that engage them with the cognitive aspects of the material, but also with their feelings and reactions (Barton & Levstik, 2003). Figure 2.1 provides several "how to" tips for Stage 1 of CPV implementation.

Figure 2.1. "How to" Tips for Stage 1 of CPV Implementation

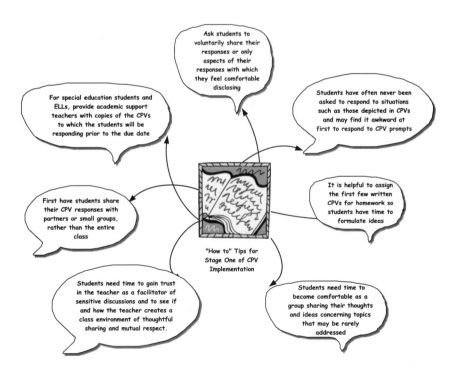

MIDDLE SCHOOL STUDENTS RESPONDING TO "BEHAVIORAL" CPVS

Teacher-created CPVs can relate to the content being taught in a particular class or lesson and/or can relate more generally to learning and communication processes themselves. Teachers have behavioral goals and expectations for their students that are just as important, if not more so, than the course content that they teach. A big part of schooling involves the socialization of students and teaching them how to act in appropriate, positive ways in various real-world situations they will encounter. One area in which all teachers want their students to excel is in their communication with peers and adults.

In middle school, students have to engage in more cooperative learning with other students and are often asked by their teachers to work in groups. The skills needed to succeed in cooperative learning groups closely mirror the kinds of skills that people need to be successful in the workplace and in various relationships in which they will be involved throughout their lives as productive adults. The CCSS share this philosophy in that they assert that helping students to be college and career ready must begin long before they graduate high school.

Example: Successful Group-Work in a 6th-Grade Classroom

The following teacher-created CPV demonstrates a 6th-grade teacher's desire to help her students participate more effectively in group-work. She used this CPV as part of her introduction to a unit on Ancient China in which students were going to be working in groups on brochures and games related to the geography of ancient China. The following introductory CPV was presented to the students to allow them to think about situations that might arise when students have to work together, outside of the monitoring of the teacher and school setting:

Students have been studying about ancient China and are working in groups on a project. The groups have been assigned by the teacher, and it turns out that you, a shy and studious person, are working with Peter, the funniest, most popular student in your class. The first time you meet at your partner Peter's house, you come up with a game plan—you are in charge of the art and half the questions, and Peter is in charge of the other half of the questions. You don't get to meet again because Peter can never make it. The week of the due date comes, and Peter says he is busy but working on the project. You decide to finish all the questions on your own, just in case. The day of your presentation, Peter shows up empty-handed, presents your work to the class, and everyone in the class loves it. What do you do? Do you tell the teacher that you did all the work? Do you speak to Peter about his lack of participation? Do you risk your friendship with Peter and consider what others might say?

This CPV encourages students to consider the value of their input in a group, as well as that of their peers by outlining a common dilemma with cooperative learning. An unfair division of group-work causes great frustration to students who work hard and have group members who do not share the group-work equitably. Sixth grade is a time when students are old enough to recognize this inherent problem with group-work and have strong opinions about how unfair this can be.

A CPV like this one offers students an opportunity to confront this potential situation before it actually occurs in the classrooms and come up with possible solutions in case it does occur. The students responded in writing to this teacher-created CPV, shared their responses verbally with the class, and created a graphic organizer depicting the positive and negative ways that students can encourage other group members to actively participate in a group project.

At the conclusion of the group portion of the ancient China unit, the students completed evaluations of themselves and their group members. Responding to the CPV in writing and the class discussion that ensued both ensured that the 6th-grade students would be more capable of filling out the evaluations of themselves and their peers more thoughtfully than they would have been able to do without having the CPV first. This teacher-created CPV might even have prevented certain problems with the ancient China group projects from occurring by spotlighting the issues surrounding group-work before commencing it.

Example: Safety in a 7th-Grade Home and Careers Class

Another example of a teacher-created CPV that dealt with behavioral concerns in the classroom was presented to 7th-grade students in a Home and Careers class. The teacher was about to begin a cooking unit in the kitchen and was beginning a lesson on kitchen safety. She presented the class with this CPV:

You and a friend are fighting over, pulling, and tugging at a knife in your cooking class. During the tussle, you and your friend both cut yourselves and are bleeding, although the cuts are small. What would you do? Would you tell the teacher and risk getting in trouble and being removed from the class? Would you not tell the teacher and hope the bleeding stops? Would you ask another teacher for a Band-Aid after class? Or would you simply take a chance and tell the teacher, hoping you don't get in trouble?

This CPV asks respondents to make decisions involving safety but also to consider the impact of peer pressure and what it means to be a good friend. Seventh grade is a time in students' lives when their friends are of utmost importance to them, and they often make poor decisions based on not wanting to lose friends. This CPV is about kitchen safety on the surface level but also deals with questions of how to deal with authority, peer pressure, and appropriate decisionmaking.

Student responses to this CPV included the following:

In this case, I would tell the teacher and hope I won't get in trouble. If I'm a good student and this is my first altercation, most likely I won't get in trouble. Also, because I don't want my cut to get infected and make the doctor amputate the hand the cut is on.

I would tell the teacher and hope I don't get in trouble because I'm bleeding and I don't know what to do. It might look like a small cut, but it can have many reactions to it.

I wouldn't mind getting in trouble because why am I fighting over a knife when I know knives are dangerous and I could just ask for another one?

The teacher was surprised at the majority of students' responses to this CPV. She believed prior to presenting the CPV that her students would hide that they were hurt to avoid getting in trouble. In presenting this behavioral CPV to her students, the teacher was able to assess their prior knowledge about this aspect of kitchen safety and was pleasantly surprised by their responses. She shared several of their written responses orally and anonymously with the class and used the CPV as a way of introducing kitchen safety that was more engaging than simply presenting the students with a list of rules and admonishments. She concluded the discussion by commending the class for responding in such mature ways and assuring them that their personal safety and well-being should always supersede their fears of getting in trouble.

MIDDLE SCHOOL "BEHAVIORAL EXAMPLES" AND LINKS TO THE CCSS

Now that you have seen two examples of teacher-created CPVs that were employed by teachers for behavioral instructional purposes, see Figure 2.2 for specific links between the curricular examples presented and some of the Common Core State Standards (CCSS) for English Language Arts and Literacy that are showcased in the examples. Figure 2.2 is meant to illustrate *some* of the many connections between the CPV activities described in this chapter and their corresponding Common Core State Standards, but it is by no means representative of all of the CCSS addressed in every example. This chart is provided to assist you in seeing the multifaceted connections between CPV activities and the CCSS and how the CCSS can be achieved in their classrooms when employing the CPV pedagogical model.

As seen in Figure 2.2, CPV activities seamlessly incorporate Common Core State Standards. In addition to addressing specific CCSS, CPV activities also exemplify several of the foundational ideas and constructs of the CCSS, including the CCSS recommendation that students be given "ample opportunities to take part in a variety of rich, structured conversations—as part of a whole class, in small groups, and with a partner. Being productive members of these conversations requires that students contribute accurate, relevant information; respond to and develop what others have said; make comparisons and contrasts; and analyze and synthesize a multitude of ideas in various domains" (CCSS).

In the group-work example, students engaged in a metacognitive activity in which they were asked to reflect on their own input in a group-learning context,

Figure 2.2. Middle School "Behavioral" CPVs and Links to the CCSS

Focus on Improving Group-Work	6th Grade	Middle School "Behavioral" CPVs and Links to the CCSS
Some of the Student Performance Indicators/Objectives Addressed in the CPV Unit	*CCSS Number*	*Corresponding Common Core State Standard(s) (CCSS)*
Students responded to the CPV prompt about group-work in writing.	W.6.3	Write narratives to develop real or imagined experiences or events using effective technique, relevant descriptive details, and well-structured event sequences.
Students shared their responses verbally with the class.	SL.6.4	Present claims and findings, sequencing ideas logically and using pertinent descriptions, facts, and details to accentuate main ideas or themes; use appropriate eye contact, adequate volume, and clear pronunciation.
Students created graphic organizers depicting the positive and negative ways that students can encourage others to actively participate in a group project.	SL.6.5	Include multimedia components (e.g., graphics, images, music, sound) and visual displays in presentations to clarify information.
Students completed evaluations of themselves and their group members at the conclusion of the group project.	SL.6.1b	Follow rules for collegial discussions, set specific goals and deadlines, and define individual roles as needed.
Focus on Safety and Peer Pressure	**7th Grade**	**Middle School "Behavioral" CPVs and Links to the CCSS**
Some of the Student Performance Indicators/Objectives Addressed in the CPV Unit	*CCSS Number*	*Corresponding Common Core State Standard(s) (CCSS)*
Students responded to the CPV prompt about kitchen safety in writing.	W.7.1	Write arguments to support claims with clear reasons and relevant evidence.
	W.7.3	Write narratives to develop real or imagined experiences or events using effective technique, relevant descriptive details, and well-structured event sequences.
The teacher shared several of the students' responses anonymously with the class and commended them for their mature responses regarding kitchen safety with the intention of positively influencing future student behavior in the kitchen.	SL.7.1	Acknowledge new information expressed by others and, when warranted, modify their own views.

as well as to evaluate the input of their peers. The graphic organizers they created depicting the positive and negative ways to encourage others to participate in group projects demonstrated their careful analyses of how to be productive group members and their abilities to synthesize their ideas. This CPV activity echoes Paolo Freire's idea regarding the need for dialogue to lead to transformative action. The students did not simply discuss group productivity but also used what they learned from one another to teach and encourage others.

In the safety and peer pressure example, the teacher chose to read several of the students' responses to the CPV aloud to the class anonymously, allowing her students to listen to their classmates' responses, compare them with their ideas, and synthesize these new ideas into their own responses. This activity also asked students to weigh their own safety against the threat of getting in trouble. This links back to McLaughlin and DeVoogd's (2004) four principles of critical literacy, particularly principles 1 and 2, which state that (1) critical literacy focuses on issues of power and promotes reflection, transformation, and action; and (2) critical literacy focuses on the problem and its complexity. The CPV provided a prompt for students to consider a real-world problem before it potentially occurred in the school kitchen and to consider the best course of action in a safe environment.

HIGH SCHOOL STUDENTS RESPONDING TO "CONTENT-DRIVEN" CPVS

This section provides two examples of teacher-created CPVs that were presented to high school students. These examples, unlike the preceding two, depict CPVs that foreground objectives that are specifically aligned with course content rather than overarching behavioral objectives. These CPVs may also contain behavioral components operating in the background, but the course content objectives are of primary importance, and textual analysis is central.

Example: Suicide Explored in a 12th-Grade English Class

One topic that is very difficult for anyone to discuss, let alone high school students, is suicide. This issue is particularly sensitive to discuss in secondary schools because teachers are largely unaware of experiences that their students may have had with their own suicide attempts, mental illnesses, clinical depression, drug or alcohol addiction, anxiety, or suicidal thoughts or behaviors, either their own or those of family members and friends. A teacher might also be unaware if her students have family members who have ended their own lives; and, therefore, suicide is often a taboo subject that most teachers will avoid at all costs. To further complicate the topic of suicide, some religions condemn people for taking suicidal actions, making it even more difficult to address this topic from multiple perspectives with a culturally and religiously diverse student body. Adolescence is, however, the time in people's lives when they are the most likely to attempt or commit suicide, so it is crucial to explore this important issue with teens.

One fictional work that addresses the theme of teen suicide is the 1998 novel *The Pact,* written by Jodi Picoult. In this novel, two teenagers, Chris Harte and Emily Gold, enter into a suicide pact. We learn that the suicide pact stemmed from Emily feeling that sex with Chris felt incestuous because the teens grew up next door to one another and were best friends their whole lives. Emily's emotional turmoil was worsened when she found out that she was pregnant by Chris, and feared that their families would force them to marry. Emily felt as if she were pregnant by her brother and knew that neither of their families would understand her disgust with what they viewed as two childhood sweethearts coming together beautifully.

The Pact raises many important questions about suicide, as well as gun control, including why Emily and Chris did not seek help before entering into their pact; if suicide is ever a reasonable solution to life's challenges; why Chris's father's gun was so easily accessible to him to be used in the pact; and how the families of the two teens might have unknowingly contributed to their angst. The novel has been touted as a modern-day Shakespearean-type drama, with all of the elements that are present in *Romeo & Juliet,* but in reverse, because in *The Pact,* Chris's and Emily's parents wanted them to be a couple rather than trying to tear them apart.

An example of a teacher-created CPV that was used with 12th-grade high school students as a prereading exercise to sensitize them to the difficult issues they would encounter in *The Pact* read as follows:

Imagine that you are a good student and very popular. You are close with your family and have many friends you have known since childhood. You have some terrible personal secrets that you are keeping inside, and you do not want to reveal them to anyone because you are afraid that if you do you will hurt those you love and yourself irreparably. These secrets are tearing you apart inside, and you are having trouble sleeping, eating, and functioning normally. You feel like you are all alone and begin to have thoughts of ending your life to escape your painful secrets. You begin to think that your best option is suicide. What should you do? How can you deal with your serious personal problems without hurting others or yourself?

The student responses to and discussion of this CPV began with them questioning and brainstorming on the board what the "terrible personal secrets" could be that might cause someone to consider suicide. Some possible secrets that the students mentioned included being addicted to drugs, being pregnant out of wedlock, being in a physically abusive relationship, being HIV positive, and having terminal cancer. For each secret, students had a mature discussion of the options that one might have to seek help. They made some very astute points, such as the fact that HIV and cancer are no longer death sentences and that new treatments are being developed every day; that drug addiction and being in abusive relationships are difficult but common challenges for which one can seek specialized help; and that pregnancies can be dealt with in a variety of ways, including abortion, adoption, and marriage, to name a few. One of the most positive aspects of the students' responses was that students unanimously agreed that people are never as alone as they might think they are, and that there are always ways to reach out for help, even if it's done confidentially.

During the reading of the novel, the teacher asked two guest speakers to come talk with her students: a high school guidance counselor and a representative from a teen suicide helpline. Both speakers gave students open invitations to talk with them privately and provided them with confidential phone numbers and websites to refer to if they had suicidal thoughts or were concerned about family members or friends who seemed depressed or were behaving in ways that were troubling to them.

Because this CPV unit was being taught shortly following the school shooting at Sandy Hook Elementary School on December 14, 2012, in Newtown, Connecticut, the second sensitive issue of gun control in the United States emerged organically from the class discussions and responses. Students were outraged and fearful about the school shooting, which resulted in the deaths of 20 children and six adult staff members, and wanted to discuss the connections between Chris's easy access to his father's loaded gun and how that accessibility contributed to Emily's death. As a culminating project at the conclusion of the novel, the students listened to President Obama's December 16, 2012, speech at the Sandy Hook vigil and signed a petition at the Obama administration's "We the People" petitioning website in support of stricter gun control legislation.

Throughout the unit, the students also engaged in many literary and civic exercises, including comparing and contrasting *The Pact* with *Romeo & Juliet* in an essay, writing antisuicide and gun control poetry that was displayed on the classroom bulletin boards, and speaking to 9th-graders at their school about options to explore when dealing with painful personal issues.

Example: The Holocaust in an 11th-Grade U.S. History Class

An example of a teacher-created CPV used with high school students in an 11th-grade U.S. History class was part of the teacher's unit on World War II. This teacher chose to employ a CPV activity as part of his lessons pertaining to the Holocaust. He was struck by how many of his students had very little knowledge of how many people had been murdered in the Holocaust and began presenting the class with readings and firsthand accounts and interviews of Holocaust survivors.

One fact his students found interesting was that Adolf Hitler was elected chancellor of Germany with merely 32% of the popular vote. Several students posed questions such as, "So why didn't the people just overthrow Hitler if they didn't like him?" and "How come no one in Germany did anything about the Holocaust?" The teacher believed that a CPV would help his students develop some insight into what some Germans might have been thinking as the atrocities of the Holocaust were unfolding. His postreading CPV read as follows:

Imagine you are an average person walking through the streets of Munich. You are a hard-working, law-abiding member of the society. You have begun to hear rumors about the policies of the newly elected chancellor, Adolf Hitler. On this day, you and your family are walking to church and you see a military truck suddenly pull up to a home and the troops barge in. You and your family watch in horror as the family living there is dragged out and thrown into the truck. You later learn that the family is Jewish and the father is a prominent banker. What do you do? Whom do you tell? Should you try and get involved? Why or why not? Would it be better to say nothing? If so, how might that weigh on your conscience?

The students had already acquired some prior knowledge of the Holocaust and done some reading prior to responding to this CPV. Their previous readings included an article on the German governmental programs of the early 1900s, Hitler's rise to power, excerpts from Hitler's *Mein Kampf*, and other primary source documents containing firsthand accounts from the Holocaust. Having already obtained this information, students were able to respond to the CPV in ways that took into account what might have been going through the German citizens' minds as they were witnessing injustices being perpetrated against their neighbors, family members, friends, and fellow citizens. The discussion that resulted from the students responding to this CPV indicated that they better understood why, in many cases, Germans were complacent and that, for many, there was little they could do to stop Hitler in his quest to succeed in his "final solution."

This CPV was presented at a time in the World War II unit when students had done enough reading to be able to come up with their own burning questions about the Holocaust, two of which related to the apparent complacency of the Germans with regard to the genocide occurring in their midst. This CPV, although teacher created, really derived from the students' interactions with the course material. The teacher simply took something from his unit that the students were already grappling with and restated it for them in the form of a CPV prompt.

HIGH SCHOOL "CONTENT-DRIVEN" CPV EXAMPLES AND LINKS TO CCSS

Figure 2.3 depicts links between the 12th- and 11th-grade content-driven curricular examples presented and some of the Common Core State Standards (CCSS) for English Language Arts and Literacy that are showcased in the examples. As noted in the previous section, the chart is meant to illustrate *some* of the many connections between the various CPV activities described and their corresponding Common Core State Standards, but it by no means covers all the CCSS addressed.

As seen in Figure 2.3, content-driven CPV activities can be readily aligned with specific CCSS. Additionally, building background knowledge through CPVs before reading is comparable with the overarching CCSS recommendation to "stay within the text." At the secondary level, the building of background knowledge before reading is of great importance, both because of the complexity of the reading material and the sheer volume of new ideas to which students are exposed. Using CPVs as a prereading activity, particularly before reading complex and/or

Figure 2.3. High School "Content-Driven" CPVs and Links to the CCSS

English Example: Suicide and Gun Control in the Novel *The Pact*	12th Grade	High School "Content-Driven" CPVs and Links to the CCSS
Some of the Student Performance Indicators/Objectives Addressed in the CPV Unit	*CCSS Number*	*Corresponding Common Core State Standard(s) (CCSS)*
Students compared and contrasted the characters and plot of *The Pact* with Shakespeare's *Romeo & Juliet* in essay form, using evidence from both texts.	W.11–12.1	Write arguments and support claims in an analysis of substantive topics or texts, using valid reasoning and relevant and significant evidence.
Students had extensive small-group and whole-class discussions about suicide and gun control during their CPV unit.	SL. 11–12.1	Initiate and participate effectively in a range of collaborative discussions with diverse partners on grades 11–12 topics, texts, and issues, building on others' ideas and expressing their own clearly and persuasively.
Students created their own poetry related to the issues of suicide and gun control, using poetic devices.	W.11–12.2d	Use precise language, domain-specific vocabulary, and techniques such as metaphor, simile, and analogy to manage the complexity of the topic.
U.S. History Example: Complacency in The Holocaust	**11th Grade**	**High School "Content-Driven" CPVs and Links to the CCSS**
Some of the Student Performance Indicators/Objectives Addressed in the CPV Unit	*CCSS Number*	*Corresponding Common Core State Standard(s) (CCSS)*
Students read several texts pertaining to the Holocaust and came up with their own understandings and questions based on their reading.	RI.11–12.7	Integrate and evaluate multiple sources of information presented in different formats (e.g., visually, quantitatively) as well as in words to address a question or solve a problem.
Students responded to the CPV about witnessing injustices, making inferences based on their prior readings.	RH.11–12.3	Evaluate various explanations for actions or events and determine which explanation best accords with textual evidence, acknowledging where the text leaves matters uncertain.
Students engaged in a class discussion about why many Germans were complacent and believed they were powerless to stop Hitler.	RH.11–12.9	Integrate information from diverse sources, both primary and secondary, into a coherent understanding of an idea or event, noting discrepancies among sources.

informational texts, puts students "within the text" conceptually even before they begin reading and serves as both a motivational tool and formative assessment of prior knowledge.

CLOSING THOUGHTS ON STAGE 1 OF CPV IMPLEMENTATION

One of the most important benefits for teachers with regard to creating CPVs that relate to course content is that a CPV can take concepts that might seem foreign and far-removed to students, such as nationalism or complacency in the face of atrocities, and personalize them in ways that make them highly relatable. This is a goal of importance to all teachers but is particularly crucial as students move into middle and high school courses that are filled with many concepts that seem disconnected from students' everyday lives. CPVs that relate to such concepts in secondary classrooms can help students make text-to-self, text-to-text, and text-to-world connections that they might not be able to make without the curricular bridges, mirrors, and windows that CPVs provide.

CHAPTER 3

Stage 2 of CPV Implementation
Students Create and Exchange Their Own CPVs

Once students are familiar and comfortable with responding to teacher-created CPVs and have practiced discussing them with teachers and peers, they are ready to begin creating and exchanging their own CPVs. During Stage 2 of CPV implementation, students create and exchange their own CPVs, respond to their peers' CPVs, and share their responses in pairs, small groups, and as part of whole-class discussions.

If you choose to have students create and exchange CPVs in groups, several procedures can be used. Variations on create-and-exchange processes will be explained fully later in the chapter.

It is important that conversations about student-generated CPVs are facilitated by instructors in such a way that all voices are heard and that more vocal group members do not monopolize the conversations or force other members of the group to adhere to their cultural and/or political views. In discussing the creating and exchanging of CPVs in her 5th-grade classroom, one teacher from Jackson Heights, Queens, reported the following:

My students are at an age where they are starting to become very opinionated. Performing the Create and Exchange assignment with my students was definitely an eye opener. It taught me about my students as individuals, and taught me about their takes on more serious matters, as compared to those we discuss on a daily basis.

A 6th-grade teacher, also from Queens, New York, had this to say about her experiences with creating and exchanging CPVs:

Due to the fact that the ELA Department at my school has scripted modules (units), my students had never really seen an activity outside of the box like this. . . . The students' responses were mature and reasonable, and they referred to the text. I was surprised by this because I thought they would be going off on tangents, but it was really nice seeing their discussion evolve and them pulling evidence to support what they were saying from the text. The students' reactions were priceless because they got so worked up about their CPVs and wanted to hear all of the reasoning of their classmates. Everyone was respectful of each other's opinions, yet they still voiced what they believed in.

CRITICAL LITERACY AND INQUIRY LEARNING PROVIDE
THEORETICAL FRAMEWORKS FOR STAGE 2

During the second stage of CPV implementation, the student–teacher power relationship is transformed because by their very nature, student-created CPVs eradicate what Freire termed the banking concept of education, in which knowledge is a gift bestowed by teachers upon students whom they consider to know nothing (Freire, 1970). Rather than you, as teacher, bestowing knowledge on your students, knowledge during this stage of CPV implementation is mutually negotiated and constructed.

When students create and exchange their own CPVs, Freire's "teacher student contradiction" is reconciled because all members of the class become both teachers *and* students. This can be further accomplished if you also respond to the CPVs, but do not share your responses until the class discussions are well underway. You might also change your thinking as a result of hearing students' responses and should indicate to the class when and why you have done so. This will help students see that you are concurrently raising your own critical consciousness by engaging in dialogue and reciprocal problem posing with the class.

When students create their own CPVs and exchange them with classmates, you take on a modified role in the power structure of the class in the sense that the learning becomes much more student directed. Students shape the curriculum by bringing their own questions, concerns, and problems to the foreground for consideration by their peers.

As Freire (1970) pointed out, liberating education consists of acts of cognition, not transferals of information. When responding to CPVs, particularly those created by their own classmates, students are not passive listeners and instead become "critical co-investigators in dialogue with the teacher" (p. 62). CPVs engage participants in problem posing that leads to meaningful dialogue and, ideally, transformation and action.

Freire and other proponents of critical literacy who have expanded on his original ideas in more recent years (Apple, 2014; Freire & Macedo, 2013; Gee, 2014; Janks, 2013; Janks, Dixon, Ferreira, Granville, & Newfield, 2013; Rogers, 2013; Vasquez, 2013) believe that as students continue to engage in problem posing and problem solving that relates to both themselves and the world, they view these problem-solving challenges as part of a larger context rather than simply as theoretical exercises or questions. This will, in their view, result in increasingly critical comprehension.

This process also connects to the CCSS's recent call for students to demonstrate greater independence in their learning by being able to independently discern a speaker's key points, request clarification, ask relevant questions, build on others' ideas, articulate their own ideas, confirm that they have been understood, become self-directed learners, and effectively seek out resources to assist them, including teachers and peers. Countless literacy researchers have built and expanded on the Freirian ideals over the years (Apple, 2014; Freire & Macedo, 2013; Gee,

2014; Janks, 2013; Janks et al., 2013; Rogers, 2013, 2014; Tyner, 2014; Van Lier, 2014; Vasquez, 2013), and Maloch and Bomer (2013) recently reaffirmed these basic principles by stating, "reading and writing are mutually supportive learning processes that progress atop a supportive environment of talk, problem-solving, and intellectual negotiation with peers and teacher" (p. 442).

There is also a substantial body of related work on inquiry learning (Alfieri, Brooks, Aldrich, & Tenenbaum, 2011; Fang, Lamme, & Pringle, 2010; Kuhlthau, Maniotes, & Caspari, 2007; Levy, Thomas, Drago, & Rex, 2013), also called inquiry-based learning, discovery learning, problem-based learning, and guided inquiry, that presents a modern iteration of many of the foundational ideas of Freire and critical literacy and provides a parallel theoretical framework for CPVs. Similar to the critical literacy perspective, inquiry-based learning methods also encourage student-centered approaches in which students' inquiries shape and drive the curriculum and the teacher's roles consist primarily of modeling and facilitation.

Warner and Myers (2011) point out that when employing inquiry-based lessons, teachers are

> responsible for starting the inquiry process; promoting student dialog; transitioning between small groups and classroom discussions; intervening to clear misconceptions or develop students' understanding of content material; modeling [scientific] procedures and attitudes; and utilizing student experiences to create new content knowledge. (p. 1)

Inquiry-based learning also speaks to many more issues that relate directly to the Create-and-Exchange stage of CPV implementation, including the power of the collaborative nature of learning (Lee & Smagorinsky, 2000); the need for scaffolding in problem-based learning (Hmelo-Silver, Duncan, & Chinn, 2007); ways in which technology can enhance and augment inquiry processes for both students and teachers (McKinney, 2014); the relationships between social linguistics, literacies, and learning (Gee, 2014); the benefits of inquiry-based thematic units (Shanahan, 1997); and the need for greater interaction, awareness, autonomy, and authenticity in the language curriculum (Van Lier, 2014). Stage 2 of CPV implementation is an inquiry-based learning practice because at this stage students pose their own problems and questions and use CPVs as a means of finding solutions collectively.

GUIDELINES AND SUGGESTIONS FOR
CREATING AND EXCHANGING STUDENT CPVS

There are several things you can do to help students create and exchange their own CPVs more successfully. The most important thing to remember is that modeling is essential in contributing to students' understandings of what makes a good CPV and how to word CPVs effectively. You might begin by discussing the *Guidelines for Creating CPVs*, which appear in Chapter 1, as well as the *Avoiding Common Pitfalls & Strengthening CPV Prompts* (Figure 1.2), also found in Chapter 1. You might need to modify the language of the guidelines and suggestions to suit the age and ability levels of your students.

Students should be given opportunities to brainstorm about what makes a strong CPV versus a weak one and to talk about the various cultural and/or political factors that were present in teacher-created CPV prompts to which they have responded previously. You should emphasize that a good CPV *never* contains a clear-cut right or wrong answer and should be complex enough that respondents can approach the CPV from several viewpoints.

You can discuss with your students some of the many purposes for which CPVs can be created, including those directly related to course content and those that deal with broader social and/or behavioral goals and challenges. Again, this can be achieved through modeling and discussing with students the various purposes for which CPVs can be used. Figure 3.1 depicts a brainstorming list created by 10th-grade students about the various purposes for which CPVs can be used.

Figure 3.1. Purposes for CPVs

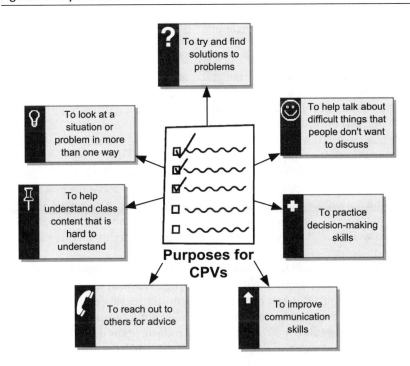

Once students understand the various purposes for which CPVs can be created, it is helpful for you to provide parameters for the type of CPV that students will create and exchange. The first time students create and exchange their own CPVs, I recommend that you be explicit about the purpose for which the CPVs are being created and exchanged.

EXAMPLE: 7TH-GRADE STUDENT CPVS ON OVERCOMING ADVERSITY AND FACING CHALLENGES

A 7th-grade language arts teacher was teaching a thematic unit about overcoming adversity. The students read several genres dealing with this overarching theme, including poetry, memoir, short story, book club books, and fiction and nonfiction selections. The teacher wanted the students to be able to make text-to-self connections to the works they had studied and to further explore the concept of adversity in their own lives and in the lives of those close to them.

She created the following CPV assignment for her students:

Please create a CPV that presents a challenge (big or small) that you have faced in your own life or one that you have seen a family member or friend face in his or her life. Be sure that the CPV explains the challenge clearly and asks for advice on how to best meet this challenge.

Student-created CPVs on overcoming adversity and facing challenges in their lives included the following:

- Imagine that you are in the 6th grade, and your parents come home from work one day and tell you that the family is moving out of state in 2 weeks. You will be leaving all of your friends and relatives to move to this new town, where you have never even visited. Your father has been transferred by his job, and the family has to move. You are shocked and upset and don't want to leave. What can you do?
- On the first day of school, you find out that your mother got a job working in the school cafeteria. She is really excited about the new job, but you are embarrassed that she is going to be working at the school and that your friends are all going to see her in the lunch room. You don't want her to work there, but you also don't want to hurt her feelings. What could you do?
- One Sunday, your father tells you that he and your mother are getting a divorce. He promises that it has nothing to do with you or your little brother and sister, and that he is going to still see you, even though he won't be living in the house with you and your mom anymore. Your best friend's parents got divorced last year, and you know that she never sees her dad anymore and that he has a new wife and baby. You are scared

and confused and feel like your life will never be the same. What should you do?

- You and your best friend always walk home from school together. One day as you are walking home he takes out a pack of cigarettes and begins smoking one. You are surprised that he is smoking, and when you ask him why he's doing it, he tells you that he's a man now and can smoke like his dad if he wants. He offers you one, and you say, "No, maybe next time." You are afraid to walk home with him again because you know he will try and give you a cigarette, and you don't want to smoke or to get in trouble for him smoking. What could you do?

In each of these CPVs, the 7th-grade students engaged in problem posing that was directly related to their thematic unit on overcoming adversity and, more important, dealt with issues that were important *to them* as individuals. Although the challenges that they chose to highlight ranged from relatively harmless issues, such as a mother working at a teen's school, to moderately serious ones, such as an adolescent being forced to move out of state or teens smoking, to quite grave ones, such as a child's fear of abandonment resulting from divorce, they were all problems for which the students themselves were seeking advice and viable solutions. Because these student-created CPVs related to personal topics, the teacher chose to have her student authors remain anonymous throughout the exchange and response processes. She had students type up their CPVs on computers and put them in a decorated shoebox on her desk without their names on them. Students were given credit for making a submission into the shoebox, but the teacher promised not to look at what the students were submitting until all of the CPVs were in the box.

Interestingly, although the teacher went to lengths to protect the student authors' identities, several chose to reveal their authorship of the CPVs during their small-group and whole-class discussions. The fact that they chose to do so voluntarily and without any encouragement from the teacher suggests that had created a nurturing classroom culture. You might recall from the end of Chapter 1 that the teacher's role in creating a supportive classroom environment for CPV activities is paramount to their success. Figure 3.2 outlines additional suggestions that can help to improve on Stage 2 of CPV implementation.

THREE VARIATIONS ON THE CREATE-AND-EXCHANGE PROCESS

The teacher reviewed the student-created CPVs and put them into three categories based on the seriousness of the challenges about which they had written. She placed all of the relatively innocuous ones in one category, such as the example involving a mom working at her child's school. The CPVs of moderate seriousness, such as the moving example, were placed into a second category, and she created a third category for very serious challenges, such as the divorce and abandonment vignette.

Figure 3.2. "How to" Tips for Creating and Exchanging Student CPVs

The teacher should
provide the students
with specific
parameters for the
content of their CPVs

The teacher should
discuss bad examples
of CPV prompts with
students and how to
repair them

The teacher should
first review the
Guidelines for
Creating CPVs with
students

When students create and
exchange personal or
sensitive CPVs, their
authorship should remain
anonymous

**"How to" Tips
for Creating &
Exchanging
Student CPVs**

Students should only
create and exchange
their own CPVs after
they have had practice
responding to teacher-
created CPV prompts

Student-created CPVs
can be exchanged with
partners, in small
groups or as a whole
class.

The First Create-and-Exchange Activity

She put the students into six groups of four and chose two of the best-written CPVs in each of the three categories of seriousness. She began by giving two of the least serious CPVs to her students. Half of the class (three small groups) received the first CPVs, and the other half (three small groups) received the second CPV. She instructed students that they should first read the CPVs silently to themselves, and then one group member should read the CPV aloud to the group. She then asked students to quietly respond in writing to their classmates' CPVs.

The teacher reminded students several times throughout the process that because these CPVs were written by other students in the class, they should not make fun of them, laugh, or ridicule one another's challenges in any way, and that if they did so there would be both academic and disciplinary repercussions. The students took the activity quite seriously and appeared engaged.

The students followed their teacher's directions and, after completing their written responses, they began small-group discussions about the challenges presented in the CPVs. They took turns reading their written responses aloud to the group and critiqued one another's responses respectfully. They were then asked to come up with a list of positive things that the person might do to help face the challenge presented by the CPV, and explain why they believed these were positive options. They were also asked to write a second list of potentially negative things the person should *not* do in this situation and explain why.

Once the groups' positive and negative lists were complete, students were asked to choose a spokesperson from each group to share their lists with the other two groups who had been given the same CPV. This reorganization essentially turned the six groups of four into two larger groups of 12. Students in the groups that had responded to the same CPV combined their individual lists and created larger master lists from them.

The language arts teacher had a teaching assistant who monitored one of the large group's discussions, while the teacher observed the other group's conversation to ensure that students were taking the assignment seriously and being respectful of each other in their discussion. The students discovered some overlap in their small-group lists, so when the new master lists were created, they were instructed to make sure there was no overlap and that all the positive and negative things that a person might do to face the challenge were included.

Next, the two large groups created mini-presentations of their CPVs and positive and negative response lists for the students in the other group who had not responded to the same CPV. The large group chose one student to read the CPV aloud to the whole class, as well as several other students to present both the positive and negative master lists they had created from their written responses to their classmates' CPVs.

Additionally, the teacher and teaching assistant selected one student from each large group to act as facilitators of a whole-class discussion on the CPVs. This student facilitator was instructed to ask the students in the other group who had not read and responded to the same CPV if they had any positive or negative suggestions to add. In both cases, the students from the other groups had additional ideas to add to their classmates' master lists. A recorder was selected in each group to add these ideas to the master lists. Finally, the activity concluded with a metacognitive whole-class discussion about the entire CPV create-and-exchange process. An excerpt from this conversation follows:

An Excerpt from a Metacognitive Student Discussion on the First CPV Create-and-Exchange Activity

---

Ms. Burrows: Before we leave class today, I would like to know your thoughts about the CPV create-and-exchange activity we did today and how you think this activity relates to the unit we have been studying on overcoming adversity.

Melinda: I was really surprised how many different ideas my group had about the same CPV. I wrote something, but then after I heard everyone else's ideas, I wanted to go back and change mine.

Scott: Yeah, me too. I didn't think of half the things that other people thought about when they answered the CPV. I only thought about it one way. I guess that's bad . . .

Ms. Burrows: One of the reasons we did our activity in groups today was so that you could share ideas, so that's perfectly fine. You were not supposed to be able to think of everything yourself! That's why we talked about our challenges in groups. Everyone has experienced different things in their lives, so no two people will look at any situation in exactly the same way.

Walter: I really liked this activity because I feel like it's thinking in real life. No offense, but we talk about a lot of fake things in this class, like characters in old stories and stuff, but this seems more like real life or even TV. I like thinking, writing, and talking about real problems.

Sam: I liked the CPV activity, too, but I liked it because it gave me ideas on what to do if I ever have the problems that we talked about today.

Ms. Burrows: You guys are so smart! That's another reason why Miss S. and I had you do this activity today. We want you to be able to practice making good decisions, so that when you have to face challenges like these in your own lives, maybe it will not be so scary because you have thought about them before and know some things that might be positive to do and others that definitely are not.

LaToya: I find that confusing. I feel like now I don't know the right answer. If there are all these choices, how is a person supposed to know what is right or wrong?

Ms. Burrows: Does anyone else also feel this way? (Several students raised their hands.) It's great that we are talking about this. Would anyone like to say anything to our classmates who find all of these choices and no right answer more confusing?

Racquel: I think that's the whole point. There is not always one right answer to a problem—it's just what's right for that person at the time. What I mean is, I think Miss B. and Miss S. want us to see that we have to make our own choices, and there are good ones and bad ones, but we have to figure it out.

Ms. Burrows: Well said! There are not right or wrong answers to the CPVs, but there are definitely better and worse choices of how to handle situations, right? You guys showed us that with your lists of positive and negative ideas. So how does this activity also relate to the literature that we have been reading the last several weeks?

Scott: Well, one way is that all of the poems and books talk about how to get over a problem, and now we are talking about our own problems, so I guess it's all about problems.

Kendra: When I read *Money Hungry*, Raspberry had to overcome being homeless and get money to keep her off the street. She did okay, even though she had big problems. Maybe the activity is supposed to relate to the literature because both show that people can do good, no matter what.

Walter: Yeah, and when I read *Tangerine*, Paul was blind, but he still really wanted to do good in his new school. He tried really hard, and he did a good job for a blind person who can't even see and stuff.

Ms. Burrows: Yes, all of the things that you mentioned are true, and those are good connections between the activity and the texts. For homework tonight, I want you to write five text-to-self connections between any of the literature that we have been studying in our adversity unit and your own lives. Tomorrow we will do another create-and-exchange CPV activity in class, using some more of your own CPVs.

In this excerpt we can see that the students did a nice job of articulating several of the intended curricular purposes of their first CPV create-and-exchange activity, as well as some of the connections between the activity and pieces of literature in their thematic unit. Although several students expressed their discomfort with the process and being faced with more than one possible correct answer to a problematic situation, the teacher was able to acknowledge and validate these students' feelings of disequilibria and call on another student, who noted that the open-ended nature of the questions was meant to represent real-life challenges and dilemmas.

The Second Create-and-Exchange Activity

The next day, the teacher did a variation of exchanging CPVs, using the CPVs that dealt with moderately serious challenges. In this activity, she had students work in pairs rather than groups and selected six of the student-created CPVs, to which the partners responded. She followed the second in-class activity up with a homework assignment that asked students to create graphic representations of their potentially positive and negative responses to the challenges discussed in the CPVs.

The next day, the teacher displayed the graphic representations around the room and had the students do a gallery walk around her classroom to look at their classmates' CPVs and graphic responses. The activity concluded with a whole-class discussion of the graphic representations and the CPVs themselves.

The Third Create-and-Exchange Activity

Finally, the teacher saved the most serious challenges CPVs for culminating activities in the unit. For these create-and-exchange activities, she selected the two most serious CPVs: the abandonment and divorce example and a second one that was particularly disturbing. The following rich example demonstrates CPVs raising students' awareness of difficult situations and inspiring transformative action, while also highlighting the importance of school personnel and community members working collaboratively.

You have an older sister who is in high school. One day, your sister is getting dressed in the bathroom, and you notice that she has cuts and scars on both of her arms. When she sees you staring at her, she quickly wraps herself up in a towel and slams the bathroom door. You are afraid to ask her why she is hurt and also scared to tell your parents or anyone else because you know your sister will be really mad at you. What do you do?

When the teacher found this anonymous CPV in the submission shoebox, she was obviously extremely concerned. Many teachers, particularly language arts and English teachers, have had similar experiences and reactions when reading poetry, journal entries, or other forms of highly personal student writing that deal with dark and potentially dangerous or lethal topics, such as physical or sexual abuse, suicidal thoughts, rape, drug abuse, prostitution, and in this case, possible self-mutilation. The teacher did what most teachers would have done in this situation. She consulted the school psychologist for advice on what to do. The issue was further complicated by the fact that the CPV had been written and submitted anonymously, so the teacher had no idea who had written it or whether it was, in fact, a real scenario or something fictitious the student had read about or seen on television.

Collaboration with Others and Parental Consent. The school psychologist assured the teacher that both she and the assistant principal would help her in coming up with a plan that might encourage the student who wrote the CPV to come forward, without betraying the teacher's trust or doing anything that would negatively affect the respectful, trusting classroom climate that the teacher had worked so hard to create from the very first day of school. The psychologist, assistant principal, and teacher decided that the best way to handle the situation was to bring in two outside people from the local community who had real expertise in the difficult subjects raised by the two CPVs that the teacher had chosen for the third create-and-exchange activity. They first invited a guest speaker who did counseling with children and adolescents whose families were undergoing divorces to speak to the students about this common problem and things they could do to help them through a painful divorce.

They contacted a second local organization that worked with teens who are fighting depression and engaging in cutting and other forms of self-mutilating behavior and also invited them to come to the class to do a brief presentation later the same week. Although the teacher was concerned that her students might be too young for a presentation on this topic, the experts assured her that they were not and that many of the patients whom they treated for depression and even self-mutilation were as young as 10 and 11.

Finally, they sent permission letters home to parents to obtain their consent for their children to hear the guest speakers' presentations and take part in the CPV activities. Two parents out of 24 chose not to allow their children to be present for the two guest speakers or take part in the subsequent CPV activities, so during those presentations, these students did language arts assignments in the school library under the librarian's supervision. They were also given additional reading and writing assignments that would substitute for the CPV activities from which they were barred by their parents. As discussed in Chapter 1, it is important for teachers to always seek parental consent when exposing children and teens to sensitive material. Obtaining parental consent significantly reduced the risk of receiving complaints about the guest speakers from parents or school administrators.

Before either of the guest speakers came to the class to give their talks, the teacher presented both CPVs to the students and had them respond in writing. She gave the divorce vignette as a homework assignment the night before the guest speaker, but gave the cutting CPV to students to complete during class. This decision was made in conjunction with the school psychologist, who felt that some students might be confused and/or upset by the self-mutilation CPV and have questions while responding.

Guest Speakers. On the day the guest speaker arrived to speak about divorce, the teacher invited students to first share their responses to the divorce CPV, but she prefaced this by saying that she would call only on those students who volunteered and wanted to share. She told students that if they didn't want to share their whole responses, they could feel free to share whichever aspects of their responses they wished. The speaker was present for the CPV class discussion, and both the teacher and speaker were pleased that many students in the class chose to share their responses, as many of them were children of divorced families, families in which parents had never married, or families with absent fathers.

Afterward, the teacher introduced the speaker as an expert in helping kids deal with abandonment and divorce, and the speaker gave a multimedia presentation. The presentation was geared toward middle school students and consisted of a brief video, lecture, and Q & A session. The students reacted positively to the speaker, asking good questions and continuing to share not only some of their experiences with abandonment and divorce but also suggestions for their classmates on ways to get through these tough challenges.

As the discussion unfolded, the teacher recorded all of the students' suggestions on the Smart Board. The speaker concluded his presentation by providing students with a list of local resources they could use that were free and accessible to them, including several web-based resources and counseling services available at the school and in their community. The student who had written the divorce CPV revealed his authorship to the teacher, the speaker, and his classmates. They commended him for bringing such an important topic with the class through his CPV. For homework that night, the teacher asked students to write one-page reactions to the presentation and class, and the students unanimously felt that this had been one of the most informative language arts classes they had ever attended.

Later that same week, the second guest speaker arrived to speak about self-mutilation. This time students had no previous exposure to the topic, and the CPV was presented to the whole class on the Smart Board. The teacher asked students to respond to the CPV in writing, but within seconds, several hands flew up, and students had questions. The teacher encouraged them to hold their questions for just a few minutes, but instructed them to write them down.

The students' questions about the CPV included the following:

- Is this CPV real or made up?
- Did the girl get into an accident, or did someone hurt her by mistake?
- Did someone attack her?
- Why wouldn't the person in the CPV just ask the sister what happened?
- Why is the person in the CPV afraid to talk to their parents?

The guest speaker introduced herself to students as a person who worked with people suffering from depression, and she asked students if they knew what that meant. Several students raised their hands and gave responses that included: "It's when a person feels really sad, like after someone dies"; "It's when you stay inside all day and don't want to eat or take a shower because you feel bad all the time"; and "It means when you don't like doing things and you think bad thoughts a lot."

The speaker thanked the students for their responses and agreed that all of these things can relate to depression. She then explained that there are many reasons why people suffer from depression, and that some of them are physical and chemical things that happen inside people's brains and that, at other times, depression can come from dealing with really sad events in life, such as losing a child or a parent. During her talk, the speaker used a PowerPoint presentation and several short video clips to illustrate her main ideas. The last part of the presentation dealt with different ways that people deal with their depression, including eating too much, not eating enough, sleeping too much, not sleeping, using drugs or alcohol, and sometimes hurting themselves physically, such as cutting or burning themselves.

When the speaker reached this part of the presentation, several students' hands shot up because they instantly made the connection between the presentation and the CPV. The students' discussion, excerpted here, reveals that students took the discussion very seriously and that their awareness of a grave problem grew significantly as a result of the CPV.

An Excerpt from the Class Discussion on Mental Illness

Guest Speaker: (begins calling on students with raised hands) Yes, young man in the red shirt.

Marcus: So are you saying that maybe the girl in the CPV cut herself on purpose? I mean, if she did, she's totally crazy, because who would do that?

Speaker: Well, it may be possible that the girl in the CPV cut herself on purpose, but if she is suffering from clinical depression, which is a real disease, then she isn't crazy at all, is she? Would you say that someone was crazy if she had a disease like cancer or AIDS? We never want to call people who are already suffering bad names, do we? Rather than crazy, we like to say that person is mentally ill or suffering from a mental illness. That takes the blame off of the person and puts it on to the disease, where it belongs.

Bryant: People cut themselves on purpose sometimes and even shoot themselves or jump off buildings and stuff. You see it on the news all the time, but maybe they do it because they are really mad that they have that disease.

Speaker: Unfortunately, people sometimes hurt themselves because they are in a lot of pain and they think that is the only way to make it stop. But that's NEVER a solution. Hurting yourself is never a good idea. There are always people who can help you—people like me.

Sheila: If that was my sister, I would definitely tell my parents. Who cares if my sister is mad? At least I would tell my mom, and then she could probably take her to the pediatrician to get some medicine for her brain to make her stop.

Speaker: That's a really smart thing that you just said. In fact, one of the ways that people who suffer from clinical depression or other mental illnesses can sometimes be treated is with medication that works on the areas of the brain that make them feel extra sad or upset. There are other treatments, too, like therapy and counseling with groups or with the patient alone.

Daphne: My aunt has that, and they gave her a lot of pills and stuff, but it didn't help her.

Teacher: Let's not talk about specific people we know by name, please, because mental and physical health are very personal topics, and people don't always want them talked about in public, with strangers. Let's just say, "Someone I know . . ." when we talk about people's personal lives. Okay?

Daphne: No problem. I get it. My bad!

Speaker: Would anyone else like to comment on the CPV?

Moraina: I read something online that said that people cut themselves because they can't feel anything, so it doesn't even hurt them like it should, but I don't get it. How come they can't feel anything? Is that because of the disease, too?

Speaker: (looking at the teacher) Wow! Your students are asking such smart questions! It's true that people who suffer from depression or other mental illnesses sometimes feel emotionally and even physically numb. They say that it's like they are in a deep fog or a bad dream and can't wake up. They also can get lots of other physical symptoms, like headaches, belly aches, ringing in their ears, unexplainable pain in parts of their bodies, and all sorts of other uncomfortable things.

Moraina: It sounds like a really bad disease.

Speaker: They can be, but they can also be treated, and many people can recover from them and live happy and healthy lives, just like [recovering from] cancer or HIV. The key is to get help before it gets too bad and the person starts hurting himself, or in really bad cases, tries to end his own life to escape the pain.

Marcus: I didn't mean to say the girl in the CPV was crazy before. I just meant that it was just really weird that she would want to cut her own arms up like that.

Speaker: I understand what you meant, and education and awareness are the keys. That's why I came to your class today—to talk about mental illness and some of the signs, symptoms, and treatments. I am going to leave a whole bunch of materials with your teacher, in case you want to learn more or know someone who may need help. I will be here for a few minutes while you are packing up, if anyone would like to come up and talk with me privately.

The Creation of the School Mental Wellness Program. At the end of her talk, the guest speaker spoke individually to several students. A few of them wanted to thank her personally for her presentation, and one of them confided in her that she had written the CPV, but that it wasn't about her real sister. She explained that she had seen an episode on Dr. Phil's talk show about mentally ill teens that cut themselves and thought it would be a good challenge to write about for her CPV because she couldn't think of anything interesting on her own. She was afraid that she was going to get into trouble with the teacher for writing it, and the speaker assured her that she wasn't, and that she was glad that it wasn't really happening in her family. She thanked the student for bringing such an important topic to the class and told her she might have helped save someone's life in doing so.

After the students left, the guest speaker, teacher, teaching assistant, school psychologist, and assistant principal debriefed about the presentation and the student's admission about creating the fictitious CPV. They realized as a result of this discussion that all the students in the middle school would benefit from guest speakers and presentations related to emotional wellness, including topics such as divorce and depression. The school was already involved in the DARE program through the local police department, which teaches students about drug and alcohol abuse, and a second program that taught AIDS awareness, but they had no programs dealing with mental health or how to cope with difficult family and emotional issues.

It was decided that this was a missing component and that presentations such as the ones that the 7th-grade students had attended on divorce and mental illness would be given to all students in grades 7 and 8 schoolwide. The school personnel and the representatives from the community organizations all believed that this was a positive outcome that had stemmed from the CPV activities, and the teacher was commended for bringing such important issues to the classroom, school, and community. The principal was also quite pleased with the new mental wellness program in her middle school and told the teacher that she felt programs such as these could be instrumental in helping to prevent future school violence and the kinds of tragedies that have taken place in recent years regarding mentally ill students hurting and killing other students and school personnel.

Connections to Critical Literacy and the CCSS. There are many connections between this 7th-grade language arts CPV unit on overcoming adversity and the basic tenets of critical literacy, including the basis of the unit involving students' own problem posing and the concept that dialogue that stemmed from this problem posing led ultimately to transformative action. Proponents of critical literacy, beginning with Freire (1970) and later Shor (2012) and McLaughlin and DeVoogd (2004) among others, have long believed that part of developing critical literacy skills in learners involves them actually *doing something* as a result of the transformations that occur from discussing and problem posing about these problems.

The creation of the school's mental wellness program is an example of a far-reaching transformative action that resulted from the students' CPV inquiries, but so are actions much smaller, such as the student who originally called the girl in the cutting CPV "crazy" and later apologized and modified his language use based on his new knowledge and awareness of and sensitivity to the challenges of the mentally ill. Another small transformation occurred when a student began discussing her aunt's struggle with mental illness, and the teacher asked students to speak about this highly personal issue without using people's names or identifying them to the class specifically. It is important to note that transformative actions that ideally result from pedagogical practices that enhance students' critical literacy through dialogue can either be quite extensive in nature or consist of smaller accomplishments, such as students' learning to use appropriate and sensitive language in particular contexts, something Freire (1970) aptly termed learning to "name the world."

In the 7th-grade language arts example, the students' own problem posing about overcoming challenges eventually led to the school adopting a new mental wellness program that can potentially help others in the school and community and perhaps prevent negative consequences stemming from untreated mentally ill students. The students' ideas moved beyond the classroom walls and were transformed into actions that were unseen positive consequences when the process first began.

In addition to the connections between this CPV unit and the pillars of critical literacy, this unit exemplifies many Common Core State Standards, integrating them seamlessly. Figure 3.3 outlines some of the CCSS addressed.

In summary, this CPV create-and-exchange unit addressed all of the 7th-grade literacy CCSS that relate to comprehension and collaboration, as well as those that address student presentation of knowledge and ideas. Additionally, many of the CCSS concerning the integration of knowledge and ideas, production and distribution of writing, and conventions of Standard English were represented in this CPV unit.

EXAMPLE: 10TH- AND 11TH-GRADE STUDENT CPVS IN GLOBAL STUDIES AND AMERICAN HISTORY

A 10th- and 11th-grade social studies teacher used student-created-and-exchanged CPVs for different curricular purposes than the 7th-grade language arts teacher

Figure 3.3. 7th-Grade Create-and-Exchange CPV Unit and Links to the CCSS

Theme: Overcoming Adversity	7th Grade	Create-and-Exchange CPV Unit and Links to the CCSS
Some of the Student Performance Indicators/ Objectives Addressed in the CPV Unit	*CCSS Number*	*Corresponding Common Core State Standard(s) (CCSS)*
Students discussed the CPVs that had been created by their classmates in pairs, small groups, larger groups, and as a whole class, articulating their opinions and changing them as a result of others' ideas.	SL.7.1	Engage effectively in a range of collaborative discussions (one-on-one, in groups, and teacher led) with diverse partners on grade-7 topics, texts, and issues, building on others' ideas and expressing their own clearly.
In their small groups and larger groups, students had to take on the roles of recorder, discussion facilitator, and others when creating their positive and negative actions lists.	SL.7.1b	Follow rules for collegial discussions, track progress toward specific goals and deadlines, and define individual goals as needed.
During discussions and creation of the lists, students changed their responses when they heard those of their classmates and incorporated their new ideas into their responses.	SL.7.1d	Acknowledge new information expressed by others and, when warranted, modify their own views.
When presenting their positive and negative lists, students had to explain not only the actions but also why they believed them to be positive or negative.	SL.7.4	Present claims and findings, emphasizing salient points in a focused, coherent manner with pertinent descriptions, facts, details, and examples.
Students created graphic representations of their classmates' CPVs, did a gallery walk, and explained their graphics to one another in class.	SL.7.5	Include multimedia components and visual displays in presentations to clarify claims and findings and to emphasize salient points.

in the previous example. The ELA teacher's primary curricular goal was to enable students to connect the literature and concepts from her thematic unit on overcoming adversity and challenges to their own lives. Conversely, the social studies teacher chose to use create-and-exchange CPV activities as part of his end-of-the-year reviews and test preparation for the New York State Regents Exams in Global Studies and American History, high-stakes exams that students must pass in New York State at the end of 10th and 11th grade, respectively, in order to graduate.

The Global Studies Regents is the exam that high school students in New York historically have the greatest difficulty passing. It covers 2 years of material, traditionally taught to students in both 9th and 10th grade, and deals with cultures and historical events largely unfamiliar and sometimes incomprehensible to American students. To further complicate the exams, both the Global and U.S. History Regents require students to read, analyze, and write about primary and secondary source documents, many of which contain antiquated and/or challenging vocabulary. The Regents refer to these as Document-Based Questions, or DBQs for short. Students' ability to integrate textual evidence successfully in their DBQ responses is paramount to them passing both exams. These social studies exams ask students to comprehend and synthesize information from various sources at very high levels.

Because both of these exams encompass a great deal of historical content that students often have difficulty remembering and comprehending, the social studies teacher believed that student-created-and-exchanged CPVs could be used effectively by students to help review their course content and to practice incorporating primary and secondary source materials and textual evidence into written responses. The teacher also believed that creating and exchanging CPVs would lend a much-needed and desired element of excitement and provide motivation for the review process by making it more engaging. He chose to employ a different variation of the create-and-exchange process than the three used in the previous 7th-grade example.

A Fourth Variation on the Create-and-Exchange Process

Although this high school teacher also broke his classes up into small groups, he chose to assign various review topics to different CPV groups. In the 10th-grade Global Studies classes, he assigned both topics related to the countries and continents that students had studied over the past 2 years, and others that dealt with overarching and recurrent historical themes. For example, he asked some groups to create CPVs about Africa, China, Japan, and Eastern Europe, whereas others created CPVs on genocide, imperialism, and child labor.

In his 11th-grade American History classes, he chose to assign CPV topics to groups based on specific time periods in American history, including the American Revolution, the Civil War, World War I, World War II, the Great Depression, and the Vietnam Conflict era. He made sure that students understood their CPVs did not have to deal specifically with the wars themselves, but any social, cultural, political, or historical issues that were taking place in the years leading up to the wars, or in the years immediately following.

The students in these social studies classes had participated in historical fiction and memoir book clubs throughout the school year, so the teacher also incorporated their book club selections into the CPV create-and-exchange activities. He did this so students would have additional practice incorporating textual evidence into written responses, a requirement not only in the New York State Regents exams but also in the CCSS and most state and professional organizations' standards for writing effectively, including those established by the National Council of Teachers of English (NCTE), the International Literacy Association (ILA), and the National Council for the Social Studies (NCSS).

The students' book club selections included *All But My Life* (1995) by Gerda Weissmann Klein, *The Things They Carried* (1990) by Tim O'Brien, *A Long Way Gone: Memoirs of a Boy Soldier* (2008) by Ishmeal Beah, and *Zlata's Diary: A Child's Life in Sarajevo* (1994) by Zlata Filipovic, to name a few.

In order to make the topic selections fair in the students' minds, the teacher had one student from each small group of three come up to his desk to choose their groups' topics from a hat. Unlike the previous teacher, who chose to keep her students' CPVs anonymous due to their personal nature, this teacher asked his students to create their CPVs with known authorship. He asked each of the three students in the group to individually create different CPVs on the chosen topics for homework, so that the next day in class each group had produced three student-created CPVs on their topics.

The next day, the students shared their CPVs with their group and discussed them. The following instructions were provided by the social studies teacher:

- Please read all the directions before beginning the activity!
- Begin by having each person read his or her CPV aloud to the group.
- After each person reads his or her CPV, briefly discuss and list all the cultural and/or political factors that might influence a person's response to the CPV. An example of a cultural factor that might influence a person's response could be his or her religion or country of origin. Examples of political factors (or sociopolitical factors) that might influence responses could be a person's political views on abortion or gun control.
- Next, please create lists of positive and negative ways in which respondents might react to the situation presented in the CPV and why you believe that each response listed is either positive or negative.
- Choose someone in the group to act as the recorder, and have that person write down the group's notes concerning each of the CPVs, including the factors involved, possible positive and negative responses, and why. This will help the group decide whether the CPV can definitely be approached in several different ways.
- As a group, please choose which CPV is the best one, the one that you want to give to the rest of the class as an assignment. If you cannot decide, you may also choose to combine aspects of two or more of the CPVs to create a new, improved one. Any CPVs that are too clear-cut, confusing, or offensive should not be considered for submission to Mr. K (the teacher) and response by the class.
- The person whose CPV is chosen for the class response and discussion will be read aloud to the class by the author. If your group creates a new CPV, please choose someone to act as the group spokesperson, and read it to the class.
- Another person from the group (not the author/spokesperson) should be chosen to act as the discussion leader on the day when the class discusses

their responses to your group's CPV. This job can also be shared by two people.

- Mr. K will be making a packet for the class containing all selected student CPVs that will be distributed for response. On the day when your group's CPV is discussed, your group's discussion leader(s) will lead the class discussion of the CPV.

This CPV selection process addresses many of the CCSS for speaking and listening at the secondary level, including those that relate to students coming to discussions prepared; working with peers to promote civil, democratic discussions and decisionmaking; setting clear goals and deadlines; establishing individual roles as needed; and propelling conversations by posing and responding to questions that probe reasoning and evidence. Once the CPVs were selected by the students, compiled into a packet by the social studies teacher, and distributed for student response, additional critical literacy skills and CCSS related to reading and writing were required by the teacher's detailed assignment, which read as follows:

Please respond to your classmates' CPVs two times. The first time, please respond from your own personal perspective, but do so using evidence from a primary source document that relates to the CPV, one that we have discussed and analyzed in class. For example, if the CPV relates to personal freedoms, you might choose excerpts from the Bill of Rights to help support your response. Please incorporate a minimum of two direct quotes from the primary source document into your CPV response. Use the first-person narrative point of view and "I" in your response.

The second time you respond to the CPV, please respond from the perspective of the protagonist or author of the work of historical fiction or memoir that you read in your book club. For example, if the CPV relates to personal freedoms and you read Gerda Weissmann Klein's memoir *All But My Life,* try to respond to the CPV from her perspective as a Holocaust survivor on personal freedoms.

Again, please incorporate a minimum of two direct quotes from the historical fiction or memoir into your second CPV response. Try to find quotes from the fiction or memoir that show the author's thoughts, feelings, and/or actions that are related to the CPV. Use the narrative first-person point of view and "I" in your response. Try to write the second response as if you actually *are* the author of the historical fiction or memoir.

This assignment speaks directly to many of the CCSS for reading and writing informational texts, particularly those that relate to citing textual evidence, making inferences, determining an author's point of view, integrating and evaluating multiple sources of information presented in different formats, analyzing foundational documents of historical and literary significance, and integrating knowledge and ideas.

Student-Created CPVs in Global Studies and American History

The students in Mr. K's social studies classes created several CPVs that were re-sponded to by their classmates as part of their Regents exam reviews, including the following.

A CPV that related to the plight of child soldiers in Sierra Leone, Africa:

Imagine that you come home from school one day to find that your house has been burned down by men carrying guns, and so has most of your village. They are rounding up all the teenage boys and telling them they have two choices: join their army of rebel soldiers or be executed like your family members. You are only 12 years old and have never even held a gun before. What would you do?

A CPV discussing the way the people of the United States were politically divided over the Vietnam War:

Pretend you were a drafted soldier in the Vietnam Conflict. You come home after 2 long years of fighting and seeing many of your friends killed or injured. Instead of receiving a medal or a welcome home parade, a man with long hair and a tie-dyed shirt spits on you in the street and calls you a baby killer. Other people who see you in your military uniform have similar negative reactions to you, calling you bad names, like killer and war pig. What would you do?

A CPV depicting the struggles of Muslims in war-torn Bosnia in the 1990s:

Imagine the year is 1992, and you are a 13-year-old Bosnian living in Sarajevo. Your family's electricity is cut off, your phone is dead, and there is no running water. The only food you have is from humanitarian aid packages, some cheese and bread. Your parents cannot work, and you cannot go to school because the Serbian army is killing any Bosnians they see in the street, including kids. You must stay inside and hide all day long in the back room of your house. What would you do?

A CPV illustrating the plight of Americans during the Civil War:

You are living up North during the Civil War era and have relatives who live in the South. When the war breaks out, you are expected to fight against your family members and friends who are slave owners in the South. What would you do?

These CPVs were self-selected by students to be responded to by their peers. In responding to each of the CPVs in their Regents review packets, students had to incorporate textual evidence from two sources in order to successfully complete the assignment. Figure 3.4 depicts some of the disciplinary skills required by the CCSS that are addressed in the Global Studies and American History CPV unit.

Figure 3.4. 10th- and 11th-Grade Create-and-Exchange CPV Unit and Links to the CCSS

Theme: Overcoming Adversity	10th and 11th Grades	Create-and-Exchange CPV Unit and Links to the CCSS
Some of the Student Performance Indicators/Objectives Addressed in the CPV Unit	*CCSS Number*	*Corresponding Common Core State Standard(s) (CCSS)*
Students had to decide which primary source documents best related to the themes and concepts presented in the CPVs and analyze them accordingly.	RI.9–10	Analyze seminal U.S. documents of historical and literary significance, including how they address related themes and concepts.
Students were required to effectively integrate textual evidence from two sources into their CPV responses.	W.1	Write arguments to support claims in an analysis of substantive topics or texts, using valid reasoning and relevant and sufficient evidence.
When responding to the CPVs, students wrote detailed narratives, using the first-person point of view, to develop imagined experiences related to real events that were historically significant.	W.3	Write narratives to develop real or imagined experiences or events using effective techniques, well-chosen details, and well-structured event sequences.
Students needed to use inferences in their second responses to the CPVs in which they had to put themselves into the shoes of the characters from their book club texts.	RL.9–10	Cite strong and thorough textual evidence to support analysis of what the text says explicitly as well as inferences drawn from the text.

In conclusion, the CCSS have cross-disciplinary expectations that must be met in order for students to be considered college and career ready. As part of this cross-disciplinary focus, proponents of the CCSS advocate shared responsibility for students' literacy development within the school. Teachers of subjects other than English and language arts are expected to assist students in becoming proficient in reading, analyzing, and writing and speaking about text, particularly complex informational text across content areas.

The CPV create-and-exchange activities described in the global studies and American history courses exemplify this CCSS effort. The CCSS are not alone in advocating greater emphasis across content areas on the teaching of informational text. The 2009 reading framework of the National Assessment of Educational Progress (NAEP) also requires an increasing amount of informational text for its assessment of students as they advance through the grades, as do both the NCTE and ILA Standards.

As part of their portrait of students who meet the CCSS, its authors describe students who demonstrate independence; build strong content knowledge; respond to varying demands of audience, task, purpose, and discipline; comprehend

Figure 3.5. Variations on CPV Create-and-Exchange Activities

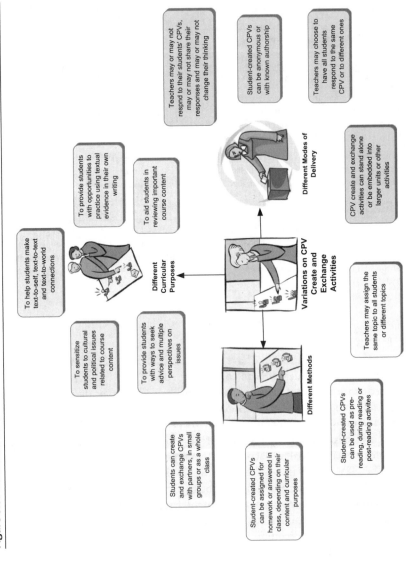

To help students make text-to-self, text-to-text and text-to-world connections

To provide students with opportunities to practice using textual evidence in their own writing

To aid students in reviewing important course content

To sensitize students to cultural and political issues related to course content

To provide students with ways to seek advice and multiple perspectives on issues

Different Curricular Purposes

Teachers may or may not respond to their students' CPVs, may or may not share their responses and may or may not change their thinking

Student-created CPVs can be anonymous or with known authorship

Teachers may choose to have all students respond to the same CPV or to different ones

Different Modes of Delivery

CPV create and exchange activities can stand alone or be embedded into larger units or other activities

Teachers may assign the same topic to all students or different topics

Variations on CPV Create and Exchange Activities

Students can create and exchange CPVs with partners, in small groups or as a whole class

Student-created CPVs can be assigned for homework or answered in class, depending on their content and curricular purposes

Student-created CPVs can be used as pre-reading, during reading or post-reading activities

Different Methods

as well as critique; value evidence; and come to understand other perspectives and cultures. The preceding CPV activities ask students to exhibit all of these same capacities of the literate individual.

CLOSING THOUGHTS ON STAGE 2 OF CPV IMPLEMENTATION

As noted in the 7th-grade language arts and 10th- and 11th-grade social studies examples included in this chapter, CPV create-and-exchange activities have many variations with regard to their curricular purposes, as well as in their methodologies and modes of delivery. Some of these variations are illustrated in Figure 3.5.

One of the most important things to take away from this chapter is that there is not one curricular purpose, methodology, or mode of delivery with regard to Stage 2 of CPV implementation in the classroom. You must decide what works best in your particular classroom, taking into consideration your students' needs and backgrounds, curricular intentions and purposes, preferences with regard to delivery, and a host of other factors, all of which have been discussed. Because CPVs are intended to be—and *are*, by nature—situated in particular learning contexts, they are always malleable so that you and your students can use them in a variety of ways.

CHAPTER 4

Stage 3 of CPV Implementation
Situated Performances of CPVs

Once students are familiar and comfortable with responding to teacher-created CPVs and creating and exchanging their own CPVs, they are ready to begin engaging in the role-playing of CPVs as situated performances. During Stage 3 of CPV implementation, students reflect on their own actions, comments, gestures, and other aspects of communication and those of their classmates and articulate the cultural, political, institutional, and interpersonal aspects of their actions as they role-play and discuss teacher and/or student-created CPV prompts.

Various techniques and strategies can be used during the situated performances of CPVs, including diverse roles that you can assume and different ways in which the student actors and audience can participate.

SITUATED COGNITION AND SITUATED PERFORMANCE PROVIDE THEORETICAL FRAMEWORKS FOR STAGE 3

Situated performance finds its theoretical roots in situated cognition research on workplace problem solving conducted during the 1980s and 1990s, which has since been taken up by literacy scholars (Lave, 1997; Purcell-Gates, Duke, & Martineau, 2007). The primary goal of this research was to gain understanding about the intricate relationships that exist between learners and the settings in which they engage in ordinary cognitive activities.

These studies examined how people problem-solve during everyday and workplace activities, outside of school. Situated cognition researchers looked at problem solving in both everyday settings (Lave, 1988, 1997; Lave & Wenger, 1991; Rogoff, 1984) and worksites (Hutchins, 1995; Scribner, 1984). Their studies yielded information concerning the natures of adaptive thinking, working intelligence, culture-specific knowledge domains (Scribner, 1984), motivation, and the ways in which learners interact with settings to effectively problem-solve.

More recently, Purcell-Gates and colleagues (2007), in a study of more than 400 2nd- and 3rd-graders, found that the most significant factor in their improvement in reading and writing informational texts was providing students with real-world reasons for engaging with them. There is nothing new about the idea that students are more motivated when they are engaged with texts for real purposes, but situated cognition researchers have delved more deeply into how and why individuals interact with their tasks, surroundings, and other factors that may improve or impede their cognitive successes.

Situated performance is an outgrowth of situated cognition and is connected to research on dramatic role-play, but it exhibits several unique characteristics. According to Finders and Rose (1999),

> Situated performances are role-taking activities with the following characteristics: (1) learners actively participate by assuming specific subject positions (as opposed to merely observing others' actions or imagining their own actions); (2) the social, cultural, institutional and interpersonal contexts for the actions and situational constraints are fore-grounded; and (3) the performed actions, motives, and circumstances are subjected to critical reflection and revision. (p. 208)

Situated performances involve acting and role-play, but also critical reflection and revision of the performed actions and dialogue. Situated performances differ from traditional role-plays because students are asked not only to reflect on their actions and other aspects of communication but are also required to identify and discuss the cultural, political, institutional, social, and relational contexts of their actions in ways that they would not in a typical role-play. Therefore, all situated performances involve role-play, but not all role-plays are situated performances. Fischer and Vander Laan (2002) pointed out that in educational contexts,

> Role-playing has a special power in that it allows students to place themselves in a vulnerable social position without any real threat or danger to themselves . . . they are able to discuss the causes, the pros and cons, and even the dangers and the advantages of lifestyles unlike their own. While such role playing methods often expose biases the students are shocked to find they hold, the culminating discussion allows for awareness, changes, and healing. (p. 25)

Situated performances of CPVs are especially useful for demonstrating to students how much communication is nonverbal (Darvin, 2009). By watching CPVs being acted out as situated performances, students quickly observe that the gestures, posture, intonation, and various other nonverbal characteristics of student actors are just as important, if not more so, than the words they say.

Kohl (2002) asserts that "Language is an everyday, every minute matter and nuances of inflection, tone, modulation and vocabulary are constantly in play in the interaction of students and teachers. There is an unarticulated linguistic sensibility that determines the nature and quality of interaction in the classroom" (p. 147). The sensibility to which Kohl is referring need not continue to be unarticulated. If we provide greater opportunities for students to observe, analyze, and discuss aspects of their own communication and that of others around them, then it follows that they will be better able to recognize the characteristics and subtle qualities of verbal interactions and respond accordingly.

These emphases on refining verbal and nonverbal communication clearly relate to the CCSS's demands that students be able to respond to the varying demands of audience, task, purpose, and discipline, as well as the CCSS's mandates about students valuing evidence and being able to effectively critique. While engaging in CPV situated performances, students must learn to adapt their communication styles in relation to audience, appreciate nuances in tone and connotation, be engaged and open-minded but discerning, work to understand what their peers are saying and/or intending to say, question a speaker's assumptions and premises, assess the veracity of claims and the soundness of one another's reasoning, and use relevant evidence when offering an interpretation of a text or situation. The situated performances of CPVs allow students to effectively practice all of the CCSS capacities of the literate individual and do so in a safe, supportive classroom environment where they are free to make mistakes, critique one another respectfully, and engage in meaningful dialogue.

VARIATIONS IN THE SITUATED PERFORMANCES OF CPVS

During the situated performances of CPVs, students are selected by the teacher or may self-select to play particular roles (i.e., student, teacher, parent, child, neighbor, etc.) and try to respond to the situations as they actually unfold. You may choose to allow students to have a narrator role in the situated performances or tell students that they must show, rather than tell, all aspects of the CPV response through acting and nonverbal gestures alone.

When beginning Stage 3, it is important to emphasize to students that this is a difficult activity, and that the whole point of the exercise is to allow them to practice problem solving, rehearse decisionmaking, and make mistakes in a safe, controlled environment. The other students are encouraged to support the actors in the role plays, and not to point out all the things that the actors do wrong or to poke fun.

One way to begin situated performances of the CPVs is to hand the CPV or CPVs to the student actors, give them 5 minutes to brainstorm, and then have them demonstrate brief dialogues that might occur in that particular situation. Another way to begin is to forgo the brainstorming time, begin the dialogue, and see how the student actors respond. Yet a third variation is to provide ample class time for students to create written scripts for the CPV situated performances, rehearse them, and then perform them for their classmates. The scripted method is the most effective for students with limited English proficiency, special education students, and others for whom additional practice is beneficial.

When students are working in collaborative groups on CPV situated performances, you may choose to give different CPVs to each group, the same CPV to all of the groups, or the same CPVs to more than one group. If more than one group is assigned the same CPV, students are provided with opportunities to see different interpretations of the same CPV and, therefore, different potential solutions to the same problem. Figure 4.1 illustrates some of the variations of situated performances of CPVs. You should decide which methodologies are best suited to your lesson objectives, students' needs, and curricular purposes.

Students who are watching their peers perform—the "audience members"—can participate in situated performances of CPVs in several ways. You can enable audience members to respond to the actors during the actual performances by pausing the dialogue and soliciting verbal comments or asking students to write comments (anonymously, if desired) on index cards that can later be shared with the actors or the entire class. An interesting addition to the situated performances is to ask a second group of student actors to challenge the first by responding to the same CPV in a different manner and then asking the class to compare and contrast the two resulting performances and their potential outcomes.

You may also choose to assign tasks to the audience members during the situated performances. For example, you may ask students in the audience to look for all the positive things the actors do in the situated performance, both verbal comments and nonverbal aspects of communication, that help to ensure a positive outcome. Students may be asked to take note of these positive aspects during

Figure 4.1. Variations in the Situated Performances of CPVs

the actual performance and then expand on the notes in the form of a written reflection, graphic representation, or other written response after the performance or for homework. Conversely, you might ask students to note things that the actors do in the situated performance that might have negative consequences. These tasks keep students who are not performing at the time actively engaged and can help them practice important literacy skills, including note-taking, comparing and contrasting, and finding evidence to support claims. It is helpful to assign tasks to the audience members that inadvertently help them to fine-tune their own group's performances and enable them to view the performances from multiple perspectives. Figure 4.2 outlines several variations in audience participation during CPV situated performances.

Just as the audience's participation in situated performances can vary tremendously, so can the role of the teacher. You can act purely as a facilitator and try not to influence the performances, or you may choose to participate in ways that do influence the performances and student actors.

One possibility can involve what Weltsek (2005) calls *teacher in role*. He describes that teacher in role means that the teacher takes on an actual role in the

Figure 4.2. Variations in Audience Participation

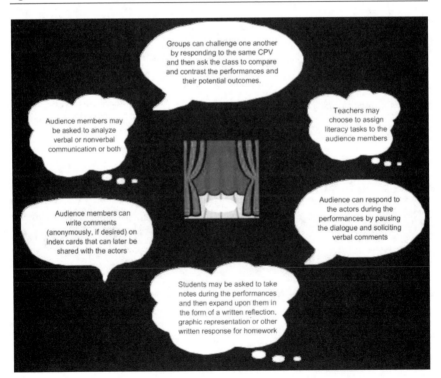

improvised world, rather than standing on the outside of the role-play and simply directing the flow of student dialogue (p. 77). He goes on to say that the teacher in role is responsible for helping the group confront issues that were identified at the beginning of the process and, when working with an outside text, looks for moments to critically connect students with that text, not to impose values or provide answers (p. 78). In situated performances of CPVs, you might take on roles in the performances themselves and assist the student-led groups in connecting the CPV prompt to a text or texts that the class has been reading.

Downy (2005) discusses employing dramatic tableaux to help students think critically about literature and real-life events. Several dramatic techniques that she describes can be successfully used in conjunction with CPV situated performances, including *spotlighting, inner monologue,* and *hot-seating.*

Downy describes spotlighting as asking a character to come to life, by perhaps touching that character on the shoulder. Then the student steps forward and responds, in character, to questions. In the case of CPV situated performances, the student who is spotlighted could be required to respond in character to questions from the teacher or from other students in the audience. The inner monologue is a second technique described by Downy for getting inside the thoughts of a character, whereby the character is released momentarily from the role-play script and asked to simply speak about whatever is on his or her mind (p. 36). Last, she describes the dramatic tool of hot-seating as "a character is released . . . and the facilitator poses questions to the character about his or her perspective or role in the conflict and then offers the character advice" (p. 36). This technique is similar to spotlighting, but in addition to asking the character questions, hot-seating allows the person posing the questions to the character to also offer advice. With CPV situated performances, rather than you, the teacher, offering the characters advice, you may choose to elicit this advice from student audience members instead.

Downy goes on to suggest that students can further develop their characters or write about what the hot-seated character could do to positively change the outcome (p. 37). The possibilities are endless in terms of the various dramatic tools that can be employed during situated performances of CPVs. Several of the variations in the role of the teacher in CPV situated performances are depicted in Figure 4.3.

EXAMPLE: INTERRACIAL DATING, RACIAL PRIDE, PROFILING, AND POLICE BRUTALITY EXPLORED IN A 9TH-GRADE ENGLISH CLASS

A 9th-grade English teacher in Long Island, New York, chose to use CPV situated performances as part of her teaching of the novel *If You Come Softly* (2010) by Jacqueline Woodson. The novel tells the story of Ellie, a young Jewish woman, and Miah, a young Black man, who meet at school and begin a romantic relationship. As their relationship progresses, the book addresses several sensitive issues, including whether the teens should tell their parents about their interracial dating

Figure 4.3. Variations in the Role of the Teacher

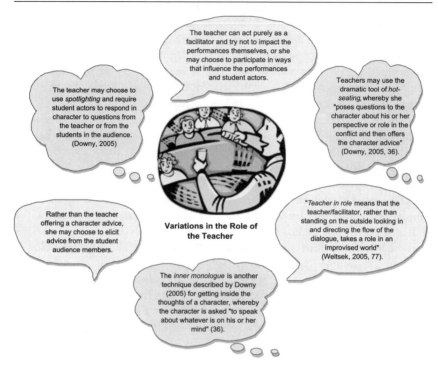

The teacher can act purely as a facilitator and try not to impact the performances themselves, or she may choose to participate in ways that influence the performances and student actors.

The teacher may choose to use *spotlighting* and require student actors to respond in character to questions from the teacher or from the students in the audience. (Downy, 2005)

Teachers may use the dramatic tool of *hot-seating*, whereby she "poses questions to the character about his or her perspective or role in the conflict and then offers the character advice" (Downy, 2005, 36).

Rather than the teacher offering a character advice, she may choose to elicit advice from the student audience members.

Variations in the Role of the Teacher

"*Teacher in role* means that the teacher/facilitator, rather than standing on the outside looking in and directing the flow of the dialogue, takes a role in an improvised world" (Weltsek, 2005, 77).

The *inner monologue* is another technique described by Downy (2005) for getting inside the thoughts of a character, whereby the character is asked "to speak about whatever is on his or her mind" (36).

relationship, the racism of people in the school and surrounding communities, people's reactions to Miah and Ellie's relationship, racial profiling, and police brutality. Prior to engaging in situated performances in class, students did several activities while reading the novel, including Sketching My Way Through the Text, a literacy strategy that asks students to draw visual representations of their understandings of particular scenes from the text (Daniels & Zemelman, 2014), and analyzing quotations from the novel for homework. The teacher then chose five excerpts from the novel that she felt were impactful and asked students to design situated performances, in small groups, around the chosen excerpts. The CPV situated performance assignment read as follows:

Each group will be provided with an excerpt from the novel *If You Come Softly*. Please create a short skit that depicts your group's interpretation of the meaning of the excerpt. The skit should not literally act out the excerpt itself, but rather your group's interpretation of what the excerpt means and what it is trying to teach people.

Before your group performs, please read your excerpt aloud to the class. After your group performs, the audience will be asked what they believe your group's interpretation of the excerpt was and why, using evidence from your skit, the novel, and any other related texts that we have studied in class.

After the audience gives their opinions about your skit, your group will have a chance to explain your actual interpretation of the excerpt and why you created the skit in the ways you did. Please prepare a written script for the skit on the computer. All group members must have speaking roles. You may also use a narrator role if you choose.

The following are the excerpts from *If You Come Softly* that the English teacher selected:

1. "He wished his grandmother was alive so he could tell her—that it wasn't a bad thing. That you couldn't get *too* black. He remembered the time his father had taken him to see a film about the Black Panthers—all those Afros and fists raised in the air. He wished his grandmother had heard them shouting, *Black is beautiful*. But she hadn't. And she had believed what she had said—that a person could get too black." (pp. 7–8)

2. "Once Anne and I were walking through Central Park when this black guy started running toward us. I frowned, remembering how Anne had screamed, and grabbed me. When the guy got up close, we realized he was a jogger, not a mugger or anything, and Anne had turned red with embarrassment. I started walking again. Would Anne have reacted that way if the man had been white?" (p. 69)

3. "'Thing about white people,' his father was saying. They were driving along the Long Island Expressway, heading out to East Hampton. There was a house his father wanted to look at for his next film. 'They don't know they're white. They know what everybody else is, but they don't know *they're* white.' He shook his head and checked his rearview mirror. 'It's strange.'" (p. 134)

4. "Ever since he was a little boy, his father had always warned him about running in white neighborhoods. Once, when he was about ten, he had torn away from his father and taken off down Madison Avenue. When his father caught up to him, he grabbed Miah's shoulder. *Don't you ever run in a white neighborhood*, he'd whispered fiercely, tears in his eyes. Then he had pulled Miah toward him and held him. *Ever.*" (p. 143)

5. "Once I asked Miah if he ever forgot he was black. *No. I never forget*, he said. *But sometimes it just doesn't matter—like I just am*. Then he asked me if I ever forgot I was white. *Sometimes*, I said. *And when you're forgetting, what color are you? No color*. Then Miah looked away from me and said, *We're different that way.*" (pp. 174–175)

Each group of four students was given one of the excerpts from the novel and time in class to discuss the excerpt and their opinions about what it meant and why. As part of the discussions that took place before the creation of the situated performances, students were also instructed to write down and discuss their text-to-self, text-to-text, and text-to-world connections to give them more ideas on how to present the excerpts as situated performances, without acting them out literally.

For example, many students had read *The Skin I'm In* (2007) by Sharon Flake earlier in the school year and were able to make connections between Miah and Maleeka Madison, the book's Black protagonist. Maleeka is a girl with self-esteem issues caused by her being bullied at school for being a very dark-skinned Black girl.

Other students made textual connections between the excerpts from *If You Come Softly* (2010) and *Face Relations: 11 Stories about Seeing beyond Color,* (2004) written by Brooklyn native Marilyn Singer, a book that they had read as part of their genre study of short story in 8th grade. This short story collection explores issues of diversity, bigotry, and racism, and includes a story about a biracial girl from Trinidad who falls in love with a boy from a different culture.

The students instantly made connections between the texts and their own lives. Several students talked about their parents not wanting them to date outside of their races or religions and expressed frustration about having to hide certain friendships and romances from them as a result of what the students termed their "old school" views.

The next day, the student groups began discussing ideas for their situated performances, based on the previous day's dialogue and the connections they had written down collectively. The following example is a script created by the group of students who received excerpt 1, in which Miah wished that his grandmother had more racial pride.

9th-Grade Situated Performance Script

Narrator: It is summer time, and it is a very hot day. All of Mandy's friends are going to the beach, but Mandy's mother does not want her to go. The following conversation occurs. . . .

Mandy: Mom, I really want to go to the beach with the other girls. Why can't I go?

Mom: Mandy, it's really hot today, and the sun is very strong. You know if you go to the beach, you're going to come home black as tar. Is that what you want?

Mandy: I don't care. What's wrong with being black? We *are* Black. I'm Black. What's the problem?

Mom: Mandy, there's being Black, and then there's being *too black. It's ugly. You know that.* Do you think those White kids are going to want to hang around you if you are really dark? You are a beautiful light-skinned Black girl. We just spent 3 hours getting your hair straightened and done, and now you want to go to the beach? No way. You can stay home and do your chores inside.

Mandy: That's crazy. I am a kid. I want to go to the beach with my friends. I don't care if my hair gets messed up or if I get darker. So what? I'm asking Dad.

Narrator: Mandy goes into her parents' bedroom and tells her father what's happening. He comes out to the kitchen to stick up for Mandy.

Dad: Mandy tells me that you don't want her to go to the beach because she will get too Black. Is that true?

Mom: I'm just looking out for her, dear. You know how mean kids can be. And, besides, we just spent all that money and time on her hair, and now she wants to ruin it!

Dad: Remember back in the day when we marched on Washington to get our civil rights? Remember how we wore our hair natural and fought and chanted, "Black is beautiful?" Was it so long ago that you already forgot?

Mom: (looking sad and embarrassed): Well, that was a long time ago, and times have changed. I just don't want my daughter to suffer and be teased like I was in school. You know how cruel girls can be at her age, honey.

Dad: If you ever want things to change in a positive way, you have to stop thinking like the ignorant bullies and let your daughter live her life as a strong Black woman, no matter how dark or light her skin is or how she wears her hair. Mandy, you have our permission and blessing to go the beach with your friends if you want.

Mandy: Thank you, Daddy. I knew you would understand.

Mom: (Smiling) Okay, fine. You two win. I'm outvoted. Just bring an umbrella and a long shirt and pants, please!

Excerpt from the Class Discussion That Followed

After the skit was performed for the class, the audience members were asked by the teacher to discuss their classmates' interpretation of the excerpt from the novel. An excerpt from the class discussion that followed the situated performance reveals that both the audience and the group benefitted from this exchange of ideas:

Ms. Chang: So now that you saw the skit, what do you think the group was trying to say? How do you think they interpreted their excerpt from the novel, and why?

Maryse: Well, they used the part about being too Black from the excerpt, but they put it into another situation by adding the beach part.

Alvin: Yeah, and the Black is beautiful part is in there, too, with the dad reminding the mom about how they stood up for their rights back in the day.

Ms. Chang: Yes, good observations! What else?

Aliya: I like how they talked about the hair part, too. I'm Black, and hair is a big thing with us! You get in trouble if you mess up your hair or your church clothes and you Black! (Students all laugh.)

Mike: I think the group wanted us to think about the racism that Black people have on each other, like the who's dark skinned and who's light skinned thing. A lot of White people don't even know that Black people treat dark-skinned Blacks worse than light-skinned Blacks. I remember my aunt not wanting my sister to marry her husband because she said he was too dark and their babies would be ugly. I was so mad!

Margaret: Maybe this is a dumb question, but if the Black people fought back in the day and believed that Black was beautiful, then what happened? Why did it go back to how it was before? Why didn't they keep being proud to be Black?

Ms. Chang: That is an excellent question—not dumb at all! Would anyone like to talk about why you believe that may have happened? Or does anyone disagree with that opinion?

Alvin: I think that it was like a fad back then to be Black, and then after a while things just went back to how they were before. Everyone forgot about the good stuff and started hating themselves again.

Greg: I think it's because, on TV, Black people are always seen as doing something bad, like killing or robbing, so TV makes people think being Black is bad.

Sally: That's true. Unless you are Obama! (Students all laugh.) But even then, they keep asking to see your birth certificate (more laughter).

Ms. Chang: Now, I would like to ask the group that created this skit to please react to what your classmates have said about your performance. Are they right about how and why you created it? Did they miss anything that you would like to add?

Group member Mary: I think they got most of it. We wanted to combine the excerpt with some of the stuff from *The Skin I'm In,* too.

Group member Alija: We also put in the part about the mom being teased for being too dark so that everyone would realize that she wasn't trying to hurt Mandy at all. She actually wanted to protect her in her own crazy way.

Group member Kareem: Yeah, she wasn't just being mean or racist. She didn't want her daughter to go through the pain she went through as a girl.

Ms. Chang: That's a really important point. Thank you for sharing that. Anything else you want to add?

Group member Mary: Yes. At the end, we put in the part about the mom telling Mandy to bring an umbrella and long shirt because we didn't want it to seem like she was just going to be all merry about the whole dark-skinned thing. What I mean is that it will take time for her to change her views, since they have been with her all her life. We wanted to show that people can change, but slowly. The mom probably will still be upset if her daughter comes home from the beach all dark and with messed up hair! (Students all laugh.)

Ms. Chang: Another *excellent* point. You guys are just so smart. You amaze me sometimes. Great job!

Other Groups' Situated Performances and Class Discussions

The other four groups' situated performances, and the class discussions that followed these performances, touched on the additional sensitive and controversial topics of interracial dating, racial profiling, and police brutality. For example, the groups that had excerpt 2 about fearing the Black jogger and excerpt 4 about never running in White neighborhoods highlighted the issues surrounding racial profiling, both by average citizens and the police. Group 2 focused on White people's views of racial profiling, whereas Group 4 tried to look at profiling from a Black perspective.

Group 4's situated performance and ensuing class discussion were particularly powerful because their excerpt was also an excellent example of the literary technique of foreshadowing. The class was learning about foreshadowing as part of their study of author's craft, so the CPV situated performance connected nicely to their understanding of this literary device.

The students also made several text-to-world and text-to-self connections as they discussed racial profiling and police brutality in the national news and in their local community. Several Latino students in the class also connected their experiences with those of Black people and described incidents of racism and profiling that they and their families had recently experienced in their Long Island community. This community is one of the few racially diverse school districts in Long Island, due to a recent influx of Latino and Caribbean immigrants.

Group 3, with the excerpt about Whites not knowing they're White, and Group 5, with the excerpt about forgetting one's color, had equally intriguing situated performances and class discussions. Their skits and talks centered on Whiteness, White identity, and White privilege, topics that are rarely addressed by adults, let alone high school students. These situated performances and conversations revolved around issues of power and what it means to be a member of a dominant or oppressed group. Many of the White students admitted that they never even considered their Whiteness in relation to non-White others or questioned why they felt "cultureless" in many respects. The English teacher used the CPV situated performances as a springboard to discuss a topic that many would consider too complex or potentially dangerous for a 9th-grade class. The students in this diverse class rose to the occasion and were able to articulate their thoughts effectively and respectfully.

The CPV situated performance activities employed in this 9th-grade English class demonstrate still more potential variations in the assignment itself, audience participation, and the role of the teacher. For this particular class and unit, the teacher chose to incorporate textual analysis, the study of literary techniques, and textual connections into CPV situated performance activities themselves.

She also modified the audience's role and gave them very specific instructions, asking them to try to discern the group's interpretation of the excerpt and the skit's underlying message or lesson. She further modified the discussion procedure by providing group members with opportunities to rebut the audience's comments if they felt they were off track and to comment on important aspects of the performances that their classmates overlooked. All of these modifications demonstrate the versatility of the CPV situated performance activities and how a teacher can contextualize the CPV activities to suit her curricular needs and the learning needs of her students.

This example also demonstrates nicely why CPV skits are defined as *situated performances* rather than traditional role-plays. You might recall that according to Finders and Rose (1999), in situated performances "the social, cultural, institutional and interpersonal contexts for the actions and situational constraints are fore-grounded," and "the performed actions, motives, and circumstances are subjected to critical reflection and revision" (p. 208). In this example, the modifications that the teacher made regarding audience participation and the actors' opportunity to respond to the audience enabled the students to critically reflect on the social, cultural, and interpersonal contexts of the situation being acted out, as well as the specifics of the performed actions, motives, and circumstances.

With regard to her role, the teacher chose to remove herself from the situated performances completely, but she facilitated and monitored the class discussions that followed quite closely and carefully. She did not use any of the dramatic techniques of spotlighting, introducing inner monologue, or hot-seating presented earlier in the chapter, but instead made a conscious choice not to interrupt the dramatic flow of the student performances in any way. With regard to the class discussion, however, she gave both the audience and student actors very specific instructions that she believed would best enable them to discuss the sensitive issues in a mature and considerate way and critically reflect on both the problems presented and the resulting performances.

9th-Grade Situated Performance Activities and Links to the CCSS

There are many ways in which the situated performance activities discussed in the *If You Come Softly* unit address the CCSS, particularly in areas that relate to key ideas and details, author's craft and structure, and the integration of knowledge and ideas. Additionally, this CPV unit is especially effective in helping students develop what the CCSS refer to as flexible communication and collaboration, in which students . . .

> must learn to work together, express and listen carefully to ideas, integrate information from oral, visual, quantitative and media sources, evaluate what they hear, use media and visual displays strategically to help achieve communicative purposes, and adapt speech to context and task. (CCSS, p. 8)

Figure 4.4 depicts some of the many CCSS addressed in this situated performance CPV unit.

Figure 4.4. 9th-Grade Situated Performance CPV Unit and Links to the CCSS

Racial Pride, Interracial Relationships, Racial Profiling, and Police Brutality	9th Grade	Situated Performance CPV Unit and Links to the CCSS
Some of the Student Performance Indicators/Objectives Addressed in the CPV Unit	*CCSS Number*	*Corresponding Common Core State Standard(s) (CCSS)*
Students had to analyze the excerpts from the novel, cite textual evidence to support their opinions, and make inferences about the excerpts and their meaning.	RL.9–19.1	Cite strong and thorough textual evidence to support analysis of what the text says explicitly as well as inferences drawn from the text.
Students discussed Woodson's use of foreshadowing at length, as well as her choice of alternating chapters with the first- and third-person points of view.	RL.9–10.5	Analyze how an author's choices concerning how to structure a text, order events within it, and manipulate time create such effects as mystery, tension, or surprise.
Students critiqued their classmates' representation of the excerpts from the text in the form of situated performances and analyzed both the written and theatrical representations of the subject/key scene.	RL.9–10.7	Analyze the representation of a subject or key scene in two different artistic mediums, including what is emphasized or absent in each treatment.
Students created their situated performances of imagined events using well-chosen details from the excerpts and sequences that made sense based on textual evidence.	W.9–10.3	Write narratives to develop real or imagined experiences or events using effective technique, well-chosen details, and well-structured event sequences.

EXAMPLE: HOMELESSNESS IN AMERICA INVESTIGATED IN A 12TH-GRADE SOCIAL STUDIES PARTICIPATION IN GOVERNMENT CLASS

A 12th-grade social studies teacher in Long Island chose to use CPV situated performance activities as part of a unit he was teaching in his Participation in Government course. This course is required of all seniors, and they must also complete 20 hours of community service hours in order to graduate, a common requirement in high schools in Long Island and throughout New York State. This social studies teacher chose to create several units throughout his course, including this one, which would enable his students to fulfill their 20 hours of required community service as natural extensions of the inquiries that they began in his class. The overarching topic that he chose to begin exploring with his students in this particular CPV unit was homelessness in America.

As part of this unit, students first examined U.S. government policies toward homelessness, beginning with the first task force on homelessness, created in 1983. They researched and examined the formation of various homeless advocacy groups, including the National Coalition for the Homeless, the National Housing Institute, and the Welfare Center. Students read, analyzed, and discussed primary source documents extensively, including the Stewart B. McKinney Act of 1987 and the more recent McKinney-Vento Homeless Education Assistance Improvements Act in the No Child Left Behind Act of 2001–2002. Students were surprised by the McKinney-Vento Act's broad definition of a homeless child as one who

> lacks a fixed, regular, and adequate nighttime residence, and who is sharing the housing of others, abandoned in hospitals, awaiting foster-care placement, or who is living in motels, hotels, trailer parks, camping grounds, cars, public places, abandoned buildings, substandard buildings, bus or train stations, or emergency or transitional shelters. (National Coalition for the Homeless, 2006)

More shocking to students were the demographic statistics regarding homelessness in America and the disparity between what came to their minds when they first thought of homelessness and the true faces of homelessness in America today. When students were originally asked to brainstorm about their views about who is homeless in America, they believed, as many Americans do, that the majority of homeless people were minority men on drugs or addicted to alcohol, concentrated in large cities like New York and Los Angeles, living on the streets, mentally ill, and often violent. They were shocked to discover that the majority of homeless people in America are, in fact, women, children, veterans, and formerly gainfully employed Americans who are residing with friends or family members, living in cars, and living in suburban and rural areas, who became homeless as a result of unaffordable housing, health issues, and/or severe poverty.

As a class, students developed the following inquiry questions based on their preliminary research: (1) What are the stereotypes regarding the homeless in America today as compared to the realities? (2) How has homelessness changed from the past until now? (3) Why do some people actually choose homelessness as a lifestyle, even when they are presented with other options? (4) Why do homeless people stay in cold cities like New York, and how do they survive the brutal winters? (5) Why do homeless people seem invisible to many people who see them every day, and how and why does this invisibility develop in American society? (6) How can we help increase awareness about homelessness in our community and help our local homeless people?

In addition to the primary source documents related to the laws surrounding homelessness, the teacher also chose to incorporate several literary texts, including excerpts from *Rachel and Her Children: Homelessness in America* by Jonathan Kozol (1988) and *The Soloist: A Lost Dream, An Unlikely Friendship, and the Redemptive Power of Music* by Steve Lopez (2008). The former is an award-winning journalistic investigation into homelessness in America in 1988, and the latter is a 2008 portrait of Nathaniel Ayers, a mentally ill cello prodigy who chose homelessness as a way of life. This book is based on a true story of a relationship between Steve Lopez, a Los Angeles reporter, and Ayers, a homeless musical genius. The students also watched the 2009 film version of *The Soloist*, staring Jamie Foxx and Robert Downey, Jr.

Other supplemental texts from which excerpts were read by the class included *Open Our Eyes: Seeing the Invisible People of Homelessness* by Kevin D. Hendricks (2010), *Living at the Edge of the World: How I Survived in the Tunnels of Grand Central Station* by Tina S. and Jamie Pastor Bolnick (2001), and *The Mole People: Life in the Tunnels Beneath New York City* by Jennifer Toth (1995).

The two books about homeless people living in the tunnels below New York City stemmed from an inquiry that the students themselves brought to the teacher about homelessness in New York City. They were profoundly curious why a homeless person would choose to remain in a cold city like New York rather than relocating to a warm climate in a place like Miami, Las Vegas, or Los Angeles, where they could sleep outside year-round without freezing to death. The first book about seeing the invisible people of homelessness was found by the students who were interested in researching how and why this state of invisibility develops in American society.

For the CPV situated performances in this unit, the teacher asked students to encapsulate the most important things that they learned while researching answers to their inquiry questions. There were six groups in the class, each with three or four student members. The students self-selected their groups based on the six inquiry questions they had developed as a class and did their research and situated performances based on their chosen inquiries.

The instructions that the students were given for their situated performances were also specific to their groups' inquiry questions.

Please create a skit that does one of the following:

- (Group/Inquiry Question 1) Compares and contrasts the stereotypes that many have regarding homeless people in America with the realities of homelessness we learned about in our research
- (Group/Inquiry Question 2) Compares and contrasts homelessness in a past era (e.g., the 1980s, the 1990s) with homelessness in America today
- (Group/Inquiry Question 3) Compares and contrasts someone being homeless voluntarily with someone being homeless due to circumstances outside of his or her control
- (Group/Inquiry Question 4) Presents some of the reasons why homeless people choose to remain in certain places and shows some of the ways in which they survive (e.g., shelters, tunnels, food banks)
- (Group/Inquiry Question 5) Presents possibilities as to why homeless people seem invisible to many people who see them every day, and how and why this invisibility develops in American society
- (Group/Inquiry Question 6) Presents ways in which we can increase awareness about homelessness in our community

Students were told to incorporate information from the primary source documents, the readings, and their research into the situated performances. When groups were performing, remaining students in the audience were instructed to take notes on their peers' performances as they pertained to the inquiry questions and on their peers' nonverbal cues. For example, when Group 1 was performing, students took notes on the stereotypes presented, as well as the realities. When Group 2 performed, the audience jotted down the qualities of homelessness that were depicted in the past era, as well as in the present. For both groups, the audience listed nonverbal aspects of communication that the actors displayed. The teacher acted as a facilitator on the day of the performances and reminded students about what they should be looking for during each performance and why.

12th-Grade Situated Performance Script

The following script was the basis for Group 2's situated performance. This group was interested in looking at the changing faces of homelessness and how homelessness in America today compares with that of the past.

Narrator: It is after midnight on a cold Thursday in January. A maintenance worker is cleaning an office building in Manhattan. He hears some noise in one of the back offices and goes to have a look.

Mr. Thomas: (looking flustered and worried) Oh, hi there, Sam. You are working real late tonight. I didn't know you were still around this late.

Sam: Hi there, Mr. Thomas. I didn't think you or anyone else would be working this late tonight, either. It sure is cold out there. How's everything? How's the family?

Mr. Thomas: I can't complain. I mean, everything has been pretty tough since my wife got sick and lost her job, but she and the kids are staying with her sister for now, so that's good. She's better off there. At least for now . . . (Mr. Thomas looks down at the floor.)

Sam: I'm sorry to hear that. Well, I wish her a speedy recovery. I'm going to let you finish up. It was really nice talking to you. Don't forget to lock up when you leave.

Mr. Thomas: Will do, Sam. You take care now.

Narrator: As Sam turns to leave, he notices something strange in Mr. Thomas's office. He sees a tooth brush, shaving cream, razor, and other personal items in a large black duffel bag. He also sees an iron and several wrinkled dress shirts lying over a chair. He dismisses it and leaves. The next day, he comes back to the office and sees Mr. Thomas. He is still in the same clothes from the night before, and Sam overhears Mr. Thomas talking on the phone as he sweeps the floor behind him.

Mr. Thomas: Sweetheart, I promise I will figure something out. I can sleep in my office and shower at the gym for now. You and the children are fine with your sister for a few weeks, while I try and work out this whole mortgage issue with the bank. There has to be some way to prevent the foreclosure. They are telling me that the house is only worth half what we paid for it in 2001 and that my income is now insufficient to remortgage. How is that possible? Anyway . . . I will work it out. I always have, and I will again.

Mrs. Thomas's voice: (from off stage) Okay, honey. I have faith in you. I just hope we can save our home somehow. What will we tell our kids? And our friends? I feel terrible about having to give our family dog away to the shelter, but how can we feed or house him? (Sobbing.) How can two middle-class, working people end up homeless like this? And what are we going to do about my medical expenses? Our health insurance only covers some of the costs of my treatments, and our bills just keep piling up. I don't know if I can even continue my treatments. . . .

Mr. Thomas: I know, honey. It's crazy, but it will all be okay. I promise. You just get better, and leave the bills and the house to me. (Mr. Thomas is shaking.)

Narrator: Sam, the janitor, is stunned to learn that Mr. Thomas, an executive at his company, is homeless and living in the office. He has read about the recent housing crisis in America and about how banks lent money to many people to buy properties that they really could not afford, but he never thought that Mr. Thomas could be one of *those people.* Mr. Thomas and his wife and children are not the kinds of people that Sam ever imagined could end up homeless. He knows that medical expenses can be thousands of dollars. As he leaves to go to the next office, Sam has a tear in his eye. He closes Mr. Thomas's door quietly and slowly shuffles down the hall, shaking his head.

In their carefully crafted situated performance, the students from Group 2 highlighted several of the many issues they had researched regarding the changing faces of homelessness today, particularly in relation to the housing and mortgage crises of 2008–2009 and their negative impacts on middle-class American families. In their skit, they also wanted to include the catastrophic effects that unforeseen medical expenses can have on families, as this was a second reoccurring theme in many of the articles they read about the causes of homelessness today, as compared to those of the past.

Additionally, Group 2 learned that the unemployment rate for Americans had gone up in recent years, leaving many previously employed Americans out of work and seeking unemployment and other government benefits that they had never formerly needed. Finally, the students in this inquiry group were saddened to learn that even animal shelters are bursting at their seams in America today because many families who could previously afford pets are no longer able to do so.

The audience members who viewed this situated performance took notes on their classmates' skit and were able to comment on the housing, medical, and pet adoption issues that were highlighted. At the conclusion of the situated performance, the teacher asked the students in the audience to share what they had observed during the skit and to ask any questions that they had for Group 2. He also requested audience members to point out all the nonverbal cues they witnessed during the situated performance, and asked them to give brief interpretations of what they believed the nonverbal cues represented in the performance and why.

Excerpt from the Class Discussion on Nonverbal Cues

Jay: Was the group exaggerating when they presented the homeless man as an executive who was living in his office and showering at the gym?

Group Member Carl: No, my brother. Unfortunately, this was not an exaggeration. It was an accurate representation of homeless middle-class people in cities across America today.

Stephanie: I see people showering at my gym and even coloring their hair, charging their phones and laptops, and eating and sleeping in the locker room. I wonder if some of them are really homeless.

Group member Ellen: Yes, it is possible that some of them are homeless.

Geneva: As far as the nonverbal cues, you could totally tell that Mr. Thomas was nervous when the janitor came through.

Mr. Merriweather: How could you tell, Geneva?

Geneva: It's easy. He was shuffling papers around on his desk, and his eyes were moving around like he was scared. When the janitor came by the office, he almost jumped out the chair!

Mr. Merriweather: Those are good observations. What else?

Kyle: You could also tell that Mr. Thomas was real upset when the janitor asked about his family. He was kind of lying when he said that he can't complain and that everyone is good and his wife is good with her sister and all that. You could tell he was lying when he looked down at the floor. People do that a lot when they're not telling the truth. I wonder if he was lying to the janitor or kind of to hisself?

Mr. Merriweather: That is a very interesting point, Kyle. Why do you ask that?

Kyle: Well, I think it was kind of both because he doesn't want anyone to know how bad things are for him and his wife, but as a man, he probably doesn't even want to admit that to hisself.

Teacher: He may not want to admit that to *himself*. That's very true. Kyle mentioned that people look down when they lie. Do you all believe that?

Sarah: No, I mean sometimes people look down or away. Sometimes they move their feet or do different things, but some people don't show any signs at all. They can look you in your eyes and lie to you and not even blink.

Mr. Merriweather: Interesting. I agree that people's nonverbal cues can be different, depending on the person.

Violet: What about at the end, when Mr. Thomas was shaking? That could be from fear or frustration or even anger.

Teacher: Yes, that is another great observation. What do you think?

Violet: I think it was all three, but him shaking shows that he was really upset and like trying to hold the feelings in, but it wasn't working, so he was shaking.

Jeff: And then at the very end, the janitor gave some nonverbal when he was . . . what was the word? Skating down the hall, shaking his head?

Mr. Merriweather: The word in the performance was *shuffling*, not *skating*.

Jeff: Right, shuffling. I think that's when you are walking slow and like dragging your feet. Since he was doing that and shaking his head at the same time, it was like he was saying to himself that Mr. Thomas's situation is real bad and hopeless. I think the janitor's nonverbal stuff showed he gave up on Mr. Thomas.

Mr. Merriweather: Does anyone disagree with Jeff's interpretation of the janitor's nonverbal cues at the end of the performance?

Kyle: No, I don't think it's that he gave up on Mr. Thomas. I think he just feels bad for him. That's why he had the tear in his eye. It's just that he probably knows how hard it is out there and all that.

Mr. Merriweather: Would any of the group members who created the performance care to respond, please?

Group member Ellen: We wanted Sam to be surprised and upset about Mr. Thomas's situation because he never would think that one of his bosses could be homeless. We weren't really saying it's hopeless. It's more like what Kyle said. We just wanted to show Sam being hurt by Mr. Thomas's situation and shaking his head in disbelief to show how shocked and upset he was.

Mr. Merriweather: These are excellent observations, class. We will continue to analyze nonverbal cues as we witness the rest of the situated performances, so please note them as you observe.

Other Groups' Situated Performances and Class Discussions

The other five groups' situated performances and the class discussions following them touched on the additional inquiry topics of (1) stereotypes regarding homeless people in America, (3) people choosing to be homeless voluntarily, (4) reasons why homeless people choose to remain in certain places and some of the ways in which they survive, (5) the invisibility of the homeless to some people, and (6) ways in which we can increase awareness about homelessness in our community.

Group 1 (stereotypes regarding homeless people in America) chose to play a dramatic trick on the audience by having one main character who had all the stereotypical qualities normally associated with homelessness in America (minority, drug addict, male, mentally ill, and violent) juxtaposed against a second main character who defied typical stereotypes of homelessness (White, female, veteran, with three young children). Throughout the performance, the audience was led to believe that the man was the homeless one, only to discover at the end of the skit that the mother of three and former navy pilot was, in fact, the one seeking permanent housing. Part of the discussion that ensued involved the literary technique of irony and how it was effectively employed in the skit.

Group 3 (people choosing to be homeless voluntarily) based much of their situated performance on Nathaniel Ayers, the homeless musical prodigy from *The Soloist,* and interviews they had read that were conducted with people who choose homelessness as a permanent way of life. They tried to emphasize the concept that society today is so complex and overwhelming that some individuals consciously choose to simply drop out of society and live an underground, alternative lifestyle. They depicted how painful this choice can be for their family members, friends, and even social workers and homeless advocates who want a healthier, safer life-style for their loved ones and cannot possibly understand why someone might choose what they view as a subhuman existence.

Group 4 (reasons why homeless people choose to remain in certain places and some of the ways in which they survive) created a skit based on what they learned from *Open Our Eyes: Seeing the Invisible People of Homelessness, Living at the Edge of the World: How I Survived in the Tunnels of Grand Central Station,* and *The Mole People: Life in the Tunnels Beneath New York City.* Their performance painted an accurate portrait of what it is like to live in the tunnels below New York City and the things that the homeless of Manhattan do to survive. Additionally, their per-formance touched on some of the reasons homeless people choose to remain in particular places, including the comfort provided by familiar settings, ties to fam-ily or community members, hopes about improving their situations in the future, and fear of the unknown.

Group 5 (the invisibility of the homeless to some people) chose to combine all three of the dramatic techniques discussed earlier in the chapter, namely spot-lighting, inner monologue, and hot-seating (Downy, 2005). In their situated per-formance, several students played homeless people lying lifelessly on the floor of a busy Manhattan train station, seemingly invisible to the crowds of commuters hurrying past them. When the narrator touched each character on the shoulder, the student actor stepped forward and responded in character to the narrator's questions about how he or she became homeless and his or her feelings about be-ing invisible to others in the station. Additionally, the inner monologue technique was used to reveal deeper thoughts and feelings of the homeless characters to the audience. They were asked by the narrator to speak about what was on their minds regarding how they had first became homeless and how they felt inside about be-ing invisible to others in society.

The dramatic tool of hot-seating was also employed. As the homeless char-acters were released by the narrator with a second touch on the shoulder, the nar-rator posed questions to the characters about their perspectives on being both homeless and invisible. The narrator offered the homeless characters advice, based on things that the students had learned through their research about the rights of the homeless and services afforded to them. The narrator also elicited advice for the homeless characters from several of the student audience members, mod-ifying and increasing the ways in which the audience members participated in this particular situated performance. Although all of the students were taught the dramatic techniques by the teacher and told they were optional additions to their situated performances, it was interesting that only Group 5 chose to employ any of the techniques, and they chose to use all three.

Finally, Group 6 (ways in which we can increase awareness about homelessness in our community) chose to center their piece around the McKinney-Vento Homeless Education Assistance Improvements Act and its possible positive impacts on homeless children in the local schools. The students were shocked to learn that in their own middle-class Long Island community, 14 students in the elementary and secondary schools were currently living in motels that served as homeless shelters, and many others were living with friends and relatives. This information was formally requested by the students from the district office in the form of a business letter and provided to the students as anonymous data.

In their skit, Group 6 chose to emphasize some of the provisions of the McKinney-Vento Act that are afforded to homeless children, including that this federal legislation requires all school districts to appoint a liaison to help communicate with homeless families and ensure that nonhoused students secure the educational services to which they are entitled.

Their group's situated performance, which was presented to their classmates last, became the basis for the follow-up community service project briefly mentioned at the beginning of this curricular example. The teacher provided an opportunity for students who wanted to continue their inquiries and work on the homeless issue to get involved with homeless issues in their local community, while concurrently fulfilling their community service requirements for graduation.

Five interested students, with the leadership of the teacher, established a 6-month tutoring program to help the homeless students in their community with their academic struggles. The students from the Participation in Government class confidentially tutored 10 students in grades 1 through 10 who were living in motels that were serving as homeless shelters in the community. They assisted these students in reading, writing, and mathematics, and also served as mentors and role models for the younger, displaced youth.

At the conclusion of the school year, the Participation in Government students were presented with special awards at graduation for their exemplary service to the community. The homeless tutoring project that began in the 12th-grade social studies classroom, and which moved seamlessly into the local community, is reminiscent of the creation of the School Mental Wellness Program from the 7th-grade example in Chapter 3. In both cases, CPV activities provided springboards for secondary students to achieve the ultimate critical literacy goal of acquiring knowledge through literacy, and then applying it to help solve a social dilemma in their local communities. Proponents of critical literacy (Apple, 2014; Freire, 1970; Freire & Macedo, 2013; Gee, 2014; Janks, 2013; Janks et al., 2013; Rogers, 2013; Vasquez, 2013) have long lamented that the most important yet commonly overlooked part of developing critical literacy skills in students involves them actually *doing* positive things in their communities as a result of the transformations that occur from engaging in problem posing and problem solving these problems in school.

12th-Grade Situated Performance Unit and Links to the CCSS

In their portrait of students who are college and career ready, the CCSS advocate that students demonstrate independence, become self-directed learners, and know how to efficiently seek out a variety of resources to assist them. Additionally, the CCSS require that students build strong content knowledge; respond to varying demands of audience, task, purpose, and discipline; comprehend as well as critique; and value evidence. This description encapsulates the very same qualities and skills that the 12th-grade students needed to be successful on the situated performance activities related to the issue of homelessness in America. Because seniors are so close to graduation, it is particularly important that they be given academic tasks that will adequately prepare them for college.

When students developed their own inquiry questions concerning homelessness in America and researched their topics in collaborative groups, they demonstrated independence, as well as their ability to seek appropriate resources, use technology, and blend online and offline learning. When they created their situated performances, they had to be acutely mindful of audience, task, and purpose, while concurrently integrating research-based content knowledge. Textual evidence was an important part of their performances as well, so that the audience could learn from their peers' performances as they pertained to the six class inquiry questions.

Because the CCSS advocate a shared responsibility for students' literacy development, there are literacy standards within the CCSS that are specific to the teaching of history/social studies, science, and technical subjects. Figure 4.5 depicts some of the links between the Reading Standards for Literacy in history/social studies grades 11–12 and the homeless unit.

REDUCING STUDENT PERFORMANCE ANXIETY

In discussing situated performance, it is important to mention the performance anxiety that students often experience and suggest some ways that you can help reduce it. Everyone experiences performance anxiety to varying degrees, and it is normal for students to be a bit anxious when they engage in situated performances in front of their peers, particularly for the first time. Secondary students are particularly susceptible to fears of looking bad in front of their peers. This is a natural part of adolescence, and it is not unusual for teenagers to be more worried about performing in front of other teenagers than adults or young children. Students' performance anxieties are compounded by the fact that they are rarely asked to "perform" in their secondary classes, unless they are taking drama courses or are involved in school plays or community theater. Because performing may be entirely new to them, you need to be prepared for performance anxiety, which might even be displayed in the form of resistance or oppositional behavior.

Figure 4.5. 12th-Grade Situated Performance CPV Unit and Links to the CCSS

Homelessness in America	12th Grade	Situated Performance CPV Unit and Links to the CCSS
Some of the Student Performance Indicators/ Objectives Addressed in the CPV Unit	*CCSS Number*	*Corresponding Common Core State Standard(s) (CCSS)*
Students analyzed several primary source documents in detail, including the McKinney-Vento Act from No Child Left Behind.	RH.11–12.5	Analyze in detail how a complex primary source is structured, including how key sentences, paragraphs, and larger portions of the text contribute to the whole.
Multiple sources of information were used in students' inquiries, including primary source documents, excerpts from literary texts, YouTube videos, and other electronic sources and databases.	RH.11–12.7	Integrate and evaluate multiple sources of information presented in diverse formats and media in order to address a question or solve a problem.
In creating their situated performances, students had to synthesized all the information they learned from diverse sources into a coherent skit that adequately presented their understanding of the inquiry topic.	RH.11–12. 9	Integrate information from diverse sources, both primary and secondary, into a coherent understanding of an idea or event, noting discrepancies among sources.
The texts that the students read in preparation for their CPV situated performances actually exceeded the complexity levels for grade 11-CCR text and were college-level readings.	RH.11–12.10	By the end of grade 12, read and comprehend history/social studies texts in the grades 11-CCR text complexity band independently and proficiently.

At the conclusion of Chapter 2, the importance of classroom culture and the teacher's role were discussed at length. You might recall that the most important factor in determining whether students will feel safe and secure expressing their thoughts and sharing their responses has to do with the classroom climate that you create during the class discussions about CPVs. Without a climate of mutual respect in the class, it is impossible to ask students to perform and share their ideas, particularly surrounding sensitive or controversial issues.

One way to help to create a climate of mutual respect and concurrently combat students' performance anxiety is for you to do several warm-up or ice-breaker activities that involve drama in your classes before asking students to engage in fully developed situated performances. Getting students accustomed to "acting" in academic classes is one way to help them feel more comfortable with both verbal self-expression and physical performance.

One example of an appropriate ice breaker is asking students to pretend to be characters from particular literary works or real people who are being studied and to have them respond to questions in character, using specific evidence from the text to support their choices with regard to their verbal answers, expressions, gestures, tone, and so on. Another good warm-up dramatic activity is to ask students to stand up and act out their interpretations of particular scenes or parts of a class text. A third possibility is to ask each student in the class to create a gesture or movement that he or she believes represents some aspect of his or her life, personality, or culture and then demonstrate the gesture and explain its significance to the class.

The possibilities are endless, and there are countless examples in drama books, but the point here is that the more the students are asked to "perform" in various ways throughout the class, the less anxious they become about doing so. Of course, if any students ridicule other students during these warm-up drama activities, it is imperative that you put a stop to the teasing immediately and discipline the students involved. It is crucial that all students know that they can take dramatic risks without fear of mockery and that if students violate the trust of their peers and you by behaving inappropriately, you will take swift action. Failure to do so may quickly result in students becoming unwilling and/or unable to fully participate in CPV situated performance activities.

For students who have learning disabilities or require additional support in the English language, and students with more severe performance anxiety caused by emotional difficulties, it is helpful for special education teachers, reading specialists, resource room teachers, ESL teachers, and other counseling and academic support staff to practice the situated performances with these students individually or in small groups before they perform them in class in front of their entire peer group. This additional scaffolding and gradual exposure reduces their performance anxiety significantly and provides them with opportunities to become more comfortable with material that might be quite challenging academically.

Although their academic needs are clearly very different, these three populations of students all benefit from additional time on task and extra practice performing in small groups before doing so in front of large groups. If for some reason some students are, or believe they are, incapable of performing in front of the whole class, it might be possible for teachers, parents, or students themselves to videotape their performances ahead of time to show to the whole class. It is important that you maintain high expectations for all your students and figure out creative ways to enable all of them to participate in CPV situated performance activities, even if they need to be tailored or modified to meet students' differing needs. Figure 4.6 summarizes the preceding suggestions for reducing student performance anxiety.

CLOSING THOUGHTS ON STAGE 3 OF CPV IMPLEMENTATION

The situated performance of CPVs is one of the most exciting aspects of CPV implementation for both you and your students. It enables your students to analyze their classmates' and their own verbal and nonverbal communication at a very high level and problem-solve. CPV situated performances can employ many different dramatic techniques and give students opportunities to practice their listening, speaking, and observation skills. When they create situated performances, students must be deeply aware of audience, task, and purpose, while concurrently integrating research-based content knowledge.

Figure 4.6. Reducing Student Performance Anxiety

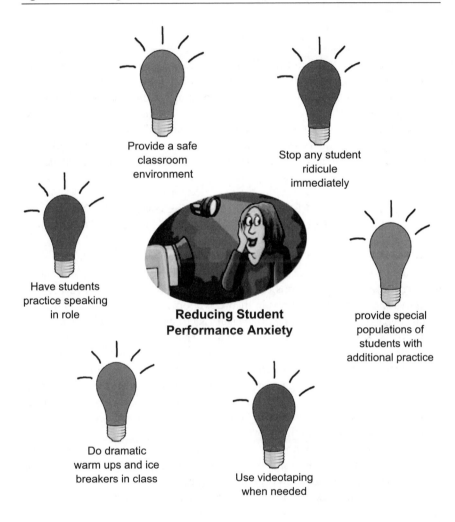

Provide a safe classroom environment

Stop any student ridicule immediately

Have students practice speaking in role

Reducing Student Performance Anxiety

provide special populations of students with additional practice

Do dramatic warm ups and ice breakers in class

Use videotaping when needed

CHAPTER 5

Stage 4 of CPV Implementation
Read and Revisit

The purpose of the Read and Revisit stage is for students and teachers to reflect on what impact, if any, reading course texts has had on their thinking, responses, and future actions, as revealed through revisiting a previously addressed CPV. This stage is an excellent way for you to assess whether the texts read and studied in class have influenced students' thinking about culturally or politically charged issues and to better understand how students are weaving their own narratives of experience by engaging with the course texts, discussions, and CPV activities.

NARRATIVES OF EXPERIENCE AND ASSESSMENT THEORY PROVIDE THEORETICAL FRAMEWORKS FOR STAGE 4

Revisiting CPVs after reading pivotal course texts gives students and teachers opportunities to engage in a multistoried process (Olson, 2000) and to simultaneously create story constellations (Craig, 2007) that can affect both their thought processes and subsequent actions in their classrooms, schools, and communities. A multistoried process is defined by Olson (2000) as one in which teacher narratives of experience profoundly and uniquely shape curriculum constructed in classrooms, and story constellations are defined by Craig (2007) as teacher narratives that are borrowed, burrowed, and "restoried" over time. From a narrative inquiry perspective, reading and revisiting CPVs can aid students and teachers in better understanding themselves, their personal metaphors, their personal practical knowledge, and how both can be applied to various problems and across situations (Connelly & Clandinin, 1988).

From an assessment standpoint, the Read and Revisit stage is the most powerful of the four stages of CPV implementation because it provides a unique type of formative assessment that allows you to see the progression of students' thinking in relation to course texts and the CPV problem-solving experience. Read-and-revisit activities advance the use of various texts and varied language experiences (Hansen, 2009), including reading, writing, listening, discussion, role-play, and more. Reading and revisiting CPVs asks students to interact with content-specific situations that engage them with the cognitive aspects of the material, but also with their feelings and reactions (Barton & Levstik, 2003).

Reading and revisiting CPVs can also be associated with Shor's (2012) classic definition of critical literacy as

[h]abits of thought, reading, writing, and speaking which go beyond surface meaning, first impressions, dominant myths, official pronouncements, traditional clichés, received wisdom, and mere opinions, to understand the deep meaning, root causes, social context, ideology, and personal consequences of any action, event, object, process, organization, experience, text, subject matter, policy, mass media, or discourse. (p. 129)

Shor (2012) posits that the core of critical literacy is about thinking in-depth, questioning official knowledge and existing authority, evaluating traditional relationships, seeking understanding of the root causes of events, and imagining how to act in order to change the conditions reflected, all of which relate directly to reading and revisiting CPVs and the development of the CCSS capacities of the literate individual.

Most students in the United States believe, because of the ways in which they are taught in our schools, that once a text has been read or a problem has been solved, there is no reason to ever return to it for further discussion. This linear, sequential style of teaching and learning permeates the U.S. school system. When using the read-and-revisit CPV approach, teaching and learning become circular and reciprocal, encouraging students to develop the deeper habits of thinking, reading, writing, and speaking to which Shor and the CCSS capacities of literate individuals refer. It is this emphasis on delving and redelving below the surface to find deeper meaning, root causes, social context, and consequences that is the theoretical earmark of reading and revisiting CPVs. In asking students to read and revisit CPVs, you can not only better assess the effect of the text on students' thinking but also better evaluate the materials you are using to prompt critical reflection.

This final stage of working with CPVs addresses many important aspects of the CCSS, particularly the Anchor Standard for Reading, Key Idea Number One: "Reading closely to determine what the text says explicitly and to make logical inferences from it; cite specific textual evidence when writing or speaking to support conclusions drawn from the text." When reading and revisiting CPVs, students must make appropriate decisions as to what they believe are the key concepts of the text, infer if and/or how these concepts relate to the CPV at hand, and then cite textual evidence as to why they would keep their responses the same or change them based on their newly acquired knowledge from the text.

One of the reasons that using textual evidence in relation to a CPV is more powerful and memorable for students than doing so in a traditional essay or paper is that it relates directly to an authentic problem-solving situation and asks them to consider and reconsider whether the textual evidence is powerful enough to motivate change in the form of real behaviors or actions. This dose of reality, when added to a traditionally academic exercise, encourages students to read texts more closely to determine what the texts say explicitly, to recognize implicit messages of each text, and to carefully consider whether the information in the texts is sufficient to motivate a change in their perceptions about the CPV and their resulting action(s). In other words, citing evidence becomes more critical when it is linked to realistic problems and potential solutions.

VARIATIONS IN DURATION OF READ-AND-REVISIT CPV ACTIVITIES

The first variation of the Read and Revisit stage of CPV implementation is as a short-term exercise in which students respond to a CPV in class (either in writing or as a situated performance), read a brief text in class or at home that night for homework, and then respond to or reperform the very same CPV again the next day. The short-term variation of read-and-revisit is especially helpful for assessing the impact that one short reading (e.g., a poem, short story, article, or excerpt from a longer work) has on students, and can help you assess students' ability to read and comprehend text independently without the benefit of any peer interaction, dialogue, or teacher input.

When students read for their own knowledge or read passages on state assessments, they do not have the benefit of interaction with others, so at times it can be helpful for you to assess their abilities to comprehend complex text independently.

A second variation at this CPV stage could be a medium-length exercise that requires both a prereading and a postreading response to a CPV based on a single, longer text. An example of this variation is a unit in which a middle school English teacher paired a CPV with the highly controversial autobiography *A Child Called It* (1995) by Dave Pelzer, a true story of one of the most horrific cases of child abuse in California history. The teacher wanted her students to think critically about the negative consequences of keeping secrets from adults, particularly those related to serious crisis situations such as abuse.

She used the following CPV as a prereading activity at the beginning of the memoir as a way to introduce the topic of child abuse and gauge her students' initial thoughts and feelings. She later did a postreading read-and-revisit and asked students to respond to the same CPV. The CPV read as follows:

Your friend calls you crying and wants to know if she can spend the night at your house. You ask your parents for permission, and they agree. When your friend comes over, she tells you that her mother got drunk again and gave her a bad beating for not doing the dishes. She begs you not to tell anyone and says that one day she is going to run away. As your friend is getting dressed for bed, you notice bad bruises on her arms and welts on her legs. What do you do? Your parents have raised you to never keep secrets from them, and you want to help your friend. You also promised never to tell anyone and don't want to betray her confidence. How can you help your friend without losing her trust?

The language arts teacher was pleasantly surprised by the unanimous changes that occurred in her students' responses to the child abuse CPV after they read from *A Child Called It* and discussed the dangers of child abuse at length as a class. All students in the class changed their CPV response and displayed greater awareness of the seriousness of child abuse. All written responses incorporated ways to anonymously assist their friend in the CPV in getting help. This CPV is an example of one that allowed the teacher to see the direct impact that the text *A Child Called It* had on her students' thinking regarding a difficult problem-solving situation.

The final option is to use read-and-revisit as a long-term exercise to demonstrate changes in students' thinking about a topic or topics over time. In this variation, after reading and deconstructing several course texts over time, students are asked to revisit their earlier responses to CPVs (written and/or performed) and decide whether they want to change them as a result of their readings and class discussions. Regardless of their decision, they must provide textual evidence to support their changes, or lack thereof, and be able to articulate how the texts support or refute their original views on the topic in particular ways.

This variation of the read-and-revisit process might occur over a period of weeks, months, or even the entire school year, as students are asked to document changes in their thinking over time and to explain specifically how course texts influenced their thinking and decisionmaking, providing detailed textual evidence and examples. This Read and Revisit stage should take place only after students are adept with responding to CPVs verbally and in writing and have engaged in both Create and Exchange (Chapter 3) and situated performances of CPVs (Chapter 4). Figure 5.1 summarizes the differences and commonalities among the variations in duration of read-and-revisit CPV activities.

It is helpful if students have prior experience with both short-term and medium-length read-and-revisit CPV activities prior to engaging in long-term read-and-revisit projects. This is because they need to understand the recursive nature of revisiting CPVs and how and why it is helpful to a learner to look back at his or her earlier understanding of a complex problem or situation. It is also recommended that you discuss explicitly with students *why* it is important to reconsider CPV prompts after reading course texts, emphasizing the importance of demonstrating as a way to measure the growth in their thinking and problem-solving abilities. Most students in the United States are not accustomed to revisiting assignments or texts in their classes, and are more familiar and comfortable with linear, sequential teaching. It is beneficial for them to gain a basic understanding and appreciation of more recursive forms of teaching and learning prior to engaging in long-term read-and-revisit activities. This will prevent students from endlessly asking you, "Why are we doing this *again*?" and being resistant to revisiting assignments and texts that they read previously and might consider completed.

The following detailed examples of long-term read-and-revisit CPV units were completed by secondary students who had this type of metacognitive conversation with teachers and classmates prior to their experiences with the units

Figure 5.1. Durations of CPV Read-and-Revisit Activities

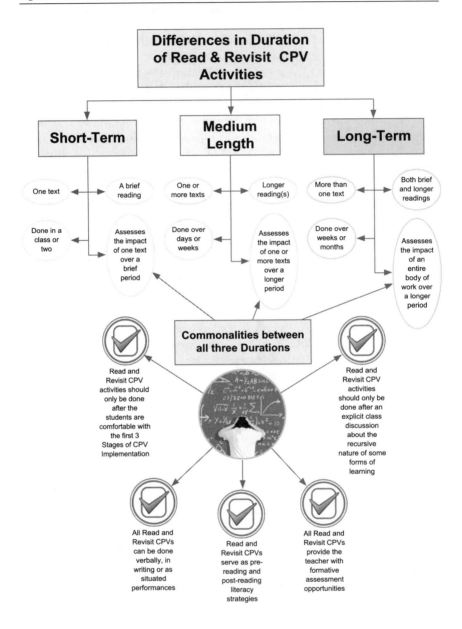

presented. These read-and-revisit CPV units were also completed after students already knew and understood how to respond to CPVs both in writing and as situated performances, and were both created and framed within larger sociocultural goals that the schools and teachers had for their students.

EXAMPLE: DATE RAPE, SEXUAL ASSAULT, AND PEER PRESSURE EXAMINED IN AN 8TH-GRADE LANGUAGE ARTS READ-AND-REVISIT UNIT

The faculty at a small suburban middle school with a diverse student population wanted to address the multitude of challenges that students face during the transitional period between middle and high school, a time when students are faced with many new academic and social challenges. Socially, they are exposed to many new people and might face unprecedented pressures by their peers to conform and be popular. Lower classmen in high school are frequently targeted by upper classmen to be physically bullied, hazed, and exposed to drugs and alcohol, sexually solicited, and a variety of other negative behaviors. The difficult transition from middle school to high school is further exacerbated if students move from a small middle school, where they were at the top of the food chain, so to speak, to a large high school, where they will be at the bottom.

The faculty at a middle school decided to design special curricula for their 8th-grade students that would help them navigate their high school transition smoothly and successfully. The curriculum was integrated and infused across a variety of 8th-grade courses, including English/language arts, social studies, health, physical education, music, art, and foreign language. Aspects of this curriculum involved teaching the 8th-graders better study skills and facts about drug and alcohol abuse, human sexuality and family planning, and a variety of other topics that teachers believed would positively influence students' decisionmaking skills upon their entry into high school.

The district had recently undergone a scandal involving alleged physical abuse of freshmen by upper classmen at the local high school, and this incident, which received media attention, was the catalyst for teachers and school administrators to carefully consider ways to better support middle school students in their transitions to high school.

One English teacher felt strongly about addressing the issue of date rape with his 8th-grade students. He strongly believed that young men are not taught about the impact that sexual assault has on women, and that young women are not taught how to avoid situations that might put them at higher risk for sexual assault or how to deal with the aftermath of sexual assault, should it occur. He was reluctant, however, to discuss the controversial topic of rape with students so young, so he sought the advice of guidance counselors and school administration before proceeding with the plan for his long-term CPV read-and-revisit unit.

Rape and Sexual Assault Statistics

In order to gain support for his unit involving date rape and the role of peer pressure in victims' responses to such assaults, the teacher began by researching the issues of rape and sexual assault in the United States. He was confronted by alarming statistics. The following statistics that he uncovered were compiled by RAINN, the Rape, Abuse, and Incest National Network, the nation's largest anti–sexual assault organizations (https://www.rainn.org/statistics):

- 44% of victims of sexual assault are under age 18, and 80% are under age 30; 15% of sexual assault and rape victims are under age 12, and 29% are ages 12 through 17.
- Approximately 66% of sexual assaults are committed by someone known to the victim, and 38% of rapists are a friend or an acquaintance; 93% of juvenile sexual assault victims know their attacker.
- Victims of sexual assault are three times more likely to suffer from depression, six times more likely to suffer from posttraumatic stress disorder, 13 times more likely to abuse alcohol, 26 times more likely to abuse drugs, and four times more likely to contemplate suicide.

The teacher used these and other statistics as a way to help persuade his colleagues and school administrators that the unit on rape is age-appropriate, that date rape is the most pressing issue to address with students, and that such a unit might have far-reaching positive consequences for students' physical and emotional health. The principal, already feeling pressure about the recent incident in the district, agreed to allow the teacher to implement the unit, but only with students whose parents signed consent forms for their children to read about and discuss these issues in class. Out of nearly 140 8th-graders in the teacher's classes, only five families asked that their children be given alternative assignments. These students were all members of strict religious groups, and their parents did not want them to be exposed to what they deemed as "adult topics" at school.

Rape and Sexual Assault Read-and-Revisit CPV Activities

At the commencement of the unit, the teacher tried to gauge his students' initial thoughts and opinions on the topics of rape, sexual assault, and peer pressure. He gave the following prereading CPV to his students to respond to in writing for homework, with very little discussion or explanation:

You are a female freshman in high school and have had the same best friend since you were in elementary school. She has been acting very strange lately, not talking to you and staying in her house all the time. When you finally pin her down and ask her what's wrong, she admits to you that she was raped at a party that you both attended during the summer, and that the boy who raped her is one of your new, very popular high school friends. She makes you promise not to tell anyone. You don't want to betray her trust. What would you do?

As a prereading activity, this CPV served as an introduction to the novel *Speak* (1999) by Laurie Halse Anderson, a National Book Award finalist, winner of eight state book awards, and finalist for 11 more. The teacher chose to use *Speak* as a whole-class novel, and to include excerpts from several fictional and nonfictional works later in the unit, including *Rape Girl* (2012) by Alina Klein, *The Trouble with Secrets* (1986) by Karen Johnsen, and *Date Rape* by Jill Hamilton (2007), to name a few.

Speak is the story of Melinda, a high school freshman who is raped by Andy, a senior, the summer before she begins high school. Melinda calls 911 from the house where the party is still occurring, but is terrified, hangs up, and runs home. The police trace the call and break up the party of underaged drinkers, arresting several people. Melinda does not tell anyone what happened with Andy and the rape. As she begins 9th grade in September, she is shunned by her peers for calling the police and turns into an immediate outcast at the high school. She becomes extremely depressed and literally stops speaking.

The day after the students responded to the *Speak* CPV in writing, the teacher asked students to create situated performances in class, based on their written responses. He put the students into groups of three or four and instructed them to share their written responses to the CPV with one another. After all students in the groups shared their written responses out loud with one another, they were told to make lists of the similarities and differences between all of their responses and to write their lists on chart paper.

They then were asked to create skits that depicted their responses to the CPVs, making sure to incorporate all of the similarities they had listed. The teacher instructed students to decide as a group which unique aspects of the group members' responses they wanted to incorporate, using only those that the group agreed to unanimously. The following script was created by one of the groups and acted out in class in the form of a situated performance.

Prereading Situated Performance Script for Speak CPV

Narrator: Cassie is a female freshman in high school and has had the same best friend, Jen, since they were in elementary school. Jen has been acting very strange lately, not talking to Cassie and staying in her house all the time. Cassie has been calling Jen, but she doesn't answer the phone. One day after school, Cassie decides to show up at Jen's house and confront her. She sees Jen walking home from the school bus and grabs her in her driveway.

Cassie: What's up, butthead? Where have you been? I've been looking for you at lunch and calling your house, but you don't answer.

Jen: (looking down) Yeah . . . well, I've been busy.

Cassie: Busy doing what? You were never too busy for me before.

Narrator: Cassie tries to tickle Jen and play around, but Jen seems upset. She suddenly bursts into tears and tells Cassie to come inside the garage so no one will hear.

Jen: Cassie, look, I have something I want to tell you, but if I do, you have to swear that you won't tell anyone.

Cassie: Jen, you know I won't. You can always trust me. You know that. We are like sisters, right?

Jen: Right. . . . Well, remember the party we went to last summer, the one when I called the police?

Cassie: Of course I do, Jen. I still really don't think you should have done that. I mean, everyone hates you now, and it's going to be really hard for you to make any new friends in high school. Everyone thinks you're a snitch. I mean, I don't, but you know what I mean. I still think that was a bad idea.

Jen: (Crying) Chris raped me, Cassie, at the party. I was so scared. I called 911, but when they answered, I freaked out and ran home. I was so confused. I didn't know what to do.

Cassie: Raped? Jen, that's a really serious thing to accuse someone of. I mean, we were all drinking, and you were wasted too, right? And everyone, including me, knows that Chris is like the hottest boy at school. He doesn't have to rape anyone. Half the girls I know would have sex with him if he wanted them to. I know you had a crush on him. What really happened?

Jen: Cassie, he raped me. We started off just talking and kissing, and then he just forced himself on me. I tried to say no, and told him to stop, but he's strong, and he was hurting me and threatening me, so I just gave in.

Cassie: Look, Jen. I'm not sure why you are saying all this crazy stuff, but I think you need to stop and put it behind you. I know you feel bad that everyone thinks you're a snitch, but they will forget over time. Maybe you should try being more friendly to people and stop being so quiet and moody.

Jen: You don't believe me?

Cassie: I'm not saying I don't believe you, but stuff happens when people are drunk. Maybe you led Chris on too much with the making out and didn't realize it. All I'm saying is that it's over and you should get on with your life. Nothing good will happen from still thinking and talking about it.

Jen: (looking down again) I guess maybe you're right.

Cassie: I know I am. I'm your best friend. I know what's best for you. I have to get going home. I'll see you tomorrow at school. Wear a new outfit and do your hair. Try and look pretty for once.

Jen: (looking down again) Okay, Cass. Sure, I will. Bye.

Narrator: When Cassie reaches home, she calls one of her new high school friends, Sandy, on the phone to tell her about Jen, breaking her promise not to talk about the secret.

Sandy: Hello?

Cassie: Hey, Sandy, this is Cass. You will never believe what Jen just told me. She said the reason she has been acting so weird and why she called the cops last summer from the party was because she was raped by Chris. Can you believe that?

Sandy: No, I don't. What a little witch. I can't believe she would lie about something like that, just because she's unpopular. Chris and I have been friends since 3rd grade, and he would never rape anyone. He has girls falling all over him. He's totally hot.

Cassie: I know. That's what I said, too. It's so sad that she's making up lies just to try and get her friends back. Anyway, I told her to just stop talking about the party and hopefully people will forget about it.

Sandy: That's good advice, Cassie. That girl Jen should be glad that she has one friend telling her the right thing to do. And she better not tell that rape story to anybody because no one will ever believe her!

Cassie: Exactly. I feel sorry for her. She used to be so much cooler when we were kids. Well, I have to go do my homework.

Sandy: Me, too! Bye.

Narrator: When Cassie hangs up the phone, she feels that she did the right thing. Sandy agreed with her that Jen is probably making up the rape story because she got drunk, had sex with Chris, and then was embarrassed after. She did not want to get in trouble for drinking, so she called the police to shut down the party.

The Class Discussion That Followed and Texts

After acting out the preceding situated performance, the students in the group that created it were asked by the teacher to explain their creative process to their classmates in the audience. They were instructed to share their chart paper containing the similarities and differences among their group members' original, written responses to the CPV and to explain how and why they created the situated performance script in the ways they did.

The students in the group discussed the fact that they all believed that Jen's rape story sounded pretty weird, and that young girls sometimes say they were sexually assaulted to avoid getting in trouble by their parents for actually having consensual sex. They felt strongly that if Jen had really been raped, she would not have hung up the phone after she dialed 911, but would have waited until police arrived to seek help and medical attention. They thought that if she had really been raped, she would have been bleeding, bruised, or cut and would have needed to go to the hospital. Additionally, all members of the group believed that a popular senior boy would have no need or motive to rape a freshman girl because they know of many girls who would have sex voluntarily with a handsome, popular older boy. One of the group members, a male student, candidly commented, "My older brother is in high school now, and he always tells me that when these chicks get drunk, they will just give it away to anyone who wants it."

This comment is a perfect example of when a teacher must steer a student-led conversation away from openly offensive statements. Although the teacher in this example did not think quickly enough to react to this misogynistic comment by the student, it would have been highly beneficial to maintaining a respectful classroom climate if he had. Although students should typically be allowed to express their opinions openly, this comment is one that, as mentioned in Chapter 1, is potentially hurtful to other students in the class, could incite violence, and might prevent other students from wanting to engage in further discussions with the offending student and others in the class. When the teacher did not respond to the comment, some students might assume that he agreed with it.

My suggestion would have been for the teacher to say something to the offending student and his classmates, such as, "Although you might be stating your or your brother's opinions, it is not appropriate for us to discuss the drinking or sexual habits of women who do not really exist or ones who do that are not here to defend themselves. This is an inappropriate, misogynistic comment and should be disregarded by the class." The teacher should have then explained to the class that misogynistic comments are ones that paint a negative picture of women and that, like racist comments, they should be excluded from academic conversations because they are potentially harmful to others.

As the other student groups acted out their situated performances and then shared aspects of their original written responses, chart papers, and group decisionmaking processes with the audience, several reoccurring and troubling themes in the students' prereading opinions regarding rape emerged. First, the overwhelming majority of the 8th-grade students seriously doubted the girl's rape story and believed that she probably just lied to avoid getting in trouble and because she was embarrassed that she had had sex. Second, they thought that the girl not seeking medical attention meant she had not been raped or physically hurt. Third, they believed that good-looking, popular guys don't rape women because they can get sex whenever they desire it. Fourth, they thought that the girl's accusations might have simply been a cry for attention to try and regain her lost friends and popularity. Finally, the students' class discussions revealed that they would not tell a parent or teacher about this situation and would choose to handle it themselves.

The teacher was shocked and appalled by many of his students' beliefs, but he tried not to reveal his horror and to allow students to experience the texts and the curricular unit he had designed for them. One of the reasons for the teacher's decision not to intervene or to reveal his own thoughts came from his firm belief in the power of inquiry learning and the need for students to uncover and discover new knowledge themselves, as part of their own inquiries and experiences. He did not want to interrupt the natural progression of the students' quest for new knowledge, so he chose to remain outwardly neutral, and although it was difficult for him to give up some of his control over the day-to-day aspects of the curriculum, he did so in the hope that the way that he designed the CPV unit would result in big changes in their thinking about rape, date rape, and sexual assault.

Over the next 2 months, students read the novel *Speak* as a whole class, as well as excerpts from several other fiction and nonfiction works that deal with the themes of rape, date rape, and sexual assault. They read poetry that was written by rape survivors from around the world, some of them teens, in a poetry collection titled *Defiled Sacredness: A Collection of Poems about the Effects of Rape and Sexual Abuse on the Individual and Society* (Mensah, 2010). Students also viewed artwork created by victims of rape and sexual assault, on temporary exhibit at a local museum. They participated in an interactive sexual assault and date-rape prevention presentation given by a guest speaker at their school. This guest speaker was found through the guidance department at the school; the speaker was part of a community organization that gave frequent presentations to secondary schools in the area. Other activities in this extended CPV unit included conducting research on subtopics of interest related to rape and sexual assault, visiting online resources for rape survivors, and talking to local police in their community about sexual assault prevention, self-defense, and the need for greater reporting of sex crimes.

At the conclusion of the unit, the teacher asked the original student groups to revisit their *Speak* CPVs and to create more informed situated performances that incorporated their newly acquired knowledge of the issues of rape and sexual assault. He told students they should also prepare a group-written reflection that explained to the class, in one or two paragraphs or a bulleted list (their choice), how their *Speak* CPV responses and situated performances had changed, and why, citing evidence from the unit to support their changes. The following section contains the transcript of revisited CPV situated performance from the group whose prereading script appeared earlier in the chapter.

Postreading Situated Performance Script for Speak CPV

Narrator: Cassie is a female freshman in high school and has had the same best friend, Jen, since they were in elementary school. Jen has been acting very strange lately, not talking to Cassie and staying in her house all the time. Cassie has been calling Jen, but she doesn't answer the phone. One day after school, Cassie decides to show up at Jen's house and confront her. She sees Jen walking home from the school bus and grabs her in her driveway.

Cassie: What's up, butthead? Where have you been? I've been looking for you at lunch and calling your house, but you don't answer.

Jen: (looking down) Yeah . . . well, I've been busy.

Cassie: Busy doing what? You were never too busy for me before.

Narrator: Cassie tries to tickle Jen and play around, but Jen seems upset. She suddenly bursts into tears and tells Cassie to come inside the garage so no one will hear.

Jen: Cassie, look, I have something I want to tell you, but if I do, you have to swear that you won't tell anyone.

Cassie: Jen, you know I won't. You can always trust me. You know that. We are like sisters, right?

Jen: Right. . . . Well, remember the party we went to last summer, the one when I called the police?

Cassie: Of course I do, Jen. I still really don't think you should have done that. I mean, everyone hates you now, and it's going to be really hard for you to make any new friends in high school. Everyone thinks you're a snitch. I mean, I don't, but you know what I mean. I still think that was a bad idea.

Jen: (Crying) Chris raped me, Cassie, at the party. I was so scared. I called 911, but when they answered, I freaked out and ran home. I was so confused. I didn't know what to do.

Cassie: Oh my God, Jen. You still haven't told your parents or the police? Why not?

Jen: Cassie, I'm scared they won't believe me. You know we were all drinking, and we are underage. And Chris is a good-looking guy with lots of friends. No one will believe that he forced himself on me. They will all think I'm lying, so what's the point?

Cassie: The point is that he violated you, Jen. And who knows if he has done that to other girls before and will do it again? I understand that you're afraid, but look how keeping it inside has been hurting you. You are totally depressed, you have withdrawn from your friends and family, your grades are going down, and you don't look well. I really think you need to tell someone besides me, Jen. You need to talk to an adult, like your mom or a counselor at school, someone who will know how to help.

Jen: I don't want anyone to know, Cass. I'm so embarrassed. I can't believe I let that happen to me. I should never have been drinking, and I did kiss Chris. I feel like it was my fault.

Cassie: Jen, rape is never your fault. We learned about that at school. I understand you may need some time to think things over, but I really want you to talk to an adult about this. I won't betray your confidence, but please just think about what I said.

Jen: Okay, Cass, I will. I'll talk to you soon. And remember, I trust you!

Cassie: Okay, Jen. I'll see you tomorrow at school. Please think about what I told you. It's really important that you get help. Being sexually assaulted can have a lot of negative effects on you later on if you don't deal with the situation. I care about you, and I want you to get the help you need and deserve.

Narrator: For the next two weeks, every time Cassie saw Jen, she gently tried to persuade her to get help. Eventually, Jen broke down and went to see the school guidance counselor to talk about what had happened. Cassie went with her to support her friend, and sexual assault charges were filed with the police against Chris, the boy who had raped Jen. The other kids at school found out the real reason why Jen had called the police, and they were sorry they had treated her badly. In the end, Cassie and Jen stayed friends, and Cassie helped Jen through this bad time in her life. Chris went to jail for 7 years.

The Class Discussion That Followed and Changes

After the read-and-revisit CPV situated performances were performed at the conclusion of the unit, the group members prepared, as per the teacher's instructions, a group-written reflection that explained to the class, in a bulleted list, how their *Speak* CPV responses and situated performances had significantly changed, and why, citing evidence from the unit to support their changes.

The most obvious and important of the changes, and one that was consistent across all the student groups' revisited situated performances, was that the best friend, rather than doubting the other girl's claims about being sexually assaulted at the party, chose instead to support the victim, even though there were aspects of her story that seemed odd or unusual. The students, as part of their reasoning behind making this significant shift in their problem-solving and decisionmaking processes, spoke about the fact that Jen was showing all the same signs of depression and posttraumatic stress displayed by Melinda, the protagonist in *Speak* who had been raped. They now recognized these signs and symptoms as being typical of those who have been sexually assaulted and felt they were more sensitive to them as a result of having completed the unit. It was this new knowledge and heightened sensitivity that caused them to alter their scripts and have the best friend be more supportive.

A second change evident in the revisited situated performance of this group, and several of the others, was the best friend's decision to maintain the victim's confidence and not tell others about what had happened. The students said they wanted the victim to realize for herself that she needed to get help, so they chose to have her best friend "work on her slowly" to encourage her to seek out the help she needed. They felt that telling other kids from school, or even adults such as parents or teachers, would break the sacred trust between the two women and only serve to further alienate the victim and discourage her from seeking help.

Finally, the students all recognized that prior to completing the unit on rape and sexual assault, they had many misconceptions, particularly about who commits such crimes. The students were shocked to learn that approximately 66% of sexual assaults are committed by someone known to the victim, 38% of rapists are a friend or an acquaintance, and 93% of juvenile sexual assault victims know their attacker. Moreover, 52% of rapists are White; 22% of imprisoned rapists are married; in 33% of sexual assaults, the perpetrator was intoxicated by alcohol or drugs; and 84% of victims report the use of physical force (accessed at https://www.rainn.org/statistics).

These statistics were directly opposed to the students' beliefs prior to completing the unit. When they created their first set of situated performances, they admitted that they believed that most rapists are strangers not known by the victim, of minority status, much older than the victims, not married or in a relationship, childless, carry guns or other weapons, and are unattractive or "crazy looking." After completing the unit, however, students recognized they had a better understanding that even good-looking young men who are popular and otherwise nonviolent can be rapists or perpetrators of sex crimes. They stated that they used this new knowledge about the kinds of people who really commit sex crimes to gain support for the victim in their revisited performances. In a nutshell, they now believed that even a popular, attractive young man is capable of committing a terrible act.

As each of the groups shared their revisited performances and their reflections concerning the changes they had made and why, it was evident to the students and teachers present that the students had a much better understanding of this controversial topic. The teacher confided that the CPV read-and-revisit activities made the students' learning about a highly complex social issue more visible and their growth easier to see and assess.

8th-Grade CPV Read-and-Revisit Activities and Links to the CCSS

The preceding 8th-grade ELA read-and-revisit CPV unit on rape, sexual assault, and peer pressure has many connections to the CCSS, particularly in the areas of writing, speaking, and listening. With regard to speaking and listening—literacy skills that are often overlooked in ELA classrooms, as compared to reading and writing—the CCSS expects that 8th-grade students will engage effectively in a range of collaborative discussions with diverse partners, building on others' ideas and expressing their own ideas clearly. A slew of essential communication skills fall under this umbrella, including coming to discussions prepared; following rules for congenial discussion; tracking progress toward specific goals; defining individual roles as needed; posing questions effectively; acknowledging new information expressed by others; and, when warranted, qualifying or justifying one's own views in light of the evidence presented. In the CPV read-and-revisit rape unit, students had to display all these skills as part of revisiting their *Speak* situated performances. The students engaged in this unit also had to adapt their speech to a variety of contexts and tasks, while using appropriate eye contact, adequate volume, and clear pronunciation.

With regard to the writing CCSS for 8th-grade students, the students had to write narratives to develop imagined experiences or events, using effective technique, relevant descriptive details, and well-structured event sequences. The situated performance scripts themselves demanded students to engage and orient the audience by establishing a context, introducing a narrator and characters, and using narrative techniques such as pacing, dialogue, description, and reflection to develop experiences and events. In summation, the situated performance scripts and accompanying revisit reflections asked students to produce writing in which the development, organization, and style are appropriate to the task, audience, and purpose—all relevant and important grade-specific expectations of the CCSS. These connections with the CCSS are depicted in Figure 5.2.

EXAMPLE: UNDERSTANDING ISLAM AND PREVENTING RELIGIOUS DISCRIMINATION AND VIOLENCE AGAINST MUSLIMS IN AN 11TH-GRADE SOCIAL STUDIES READ-AND-REVISIT UNIT

A high school social studies teacher developed a CPV read-and-revisit unit for his 11th-grade U.S. history students on understanding Islam and preventing

Figure 5.2. 8th-Grade Read-and-Revisit CPV Unit and Links to the CCSS

Rape, Sexual Assault, and Peer Pressure	8th Grade	Read-and-Revisit CPV Unit and Links to the CCSS
Some of the Student Performance Indicators/ Objectives Addressed in the CPV Unit	*CCSS Number*	*Corresponding Common Core State Standard(s) (CCSS)*
Students used chart paper to map out changes they made to their situated performances and their reasons why, citing evidence from the unit to support their changes.	W.8.1b	Support claims with logical reasoning and relevant evidence, using accurate, credible sources and demonstrating an understanding of the topic or text.
In creating their situated performances, students created believable narratives based on the CPV prompt and developed those narratives in ways that made sense to the audience and were believable.	W.8.3	Write narratives to develop real or imagined experiences or events using effective technique, relevant descriptive details, and well-structured event sequences.
Students used evidence from the unit to support their reflections about the changes they made in their responses to the CPV and the reasons they made them.	W.8.9	Draw evidence from literary or informational texts to support analysis, reflection, and research.
Students needed to adapt their speech to their tasks and code-switch between their informal language in the situated performance and their use of standard English in sharing their read-and-revisit reflections.	SL.8.6	Adapt speech to a variety of contexts and tasks, demonstrating command of formal English when indicated or appropriate.

discrimination and violence against Muslims. He did so as a direct result of breaking up several racially and religiously motivated fights between students at his school in Queens and overhearing several discriminatory remarks being made by both students and faculty members about students of Middle Eastern descent.

In the aftermath of the terrorist attacks on the World Trade Center on September 11, 2001, and various other terrorist strikes nationally and internationally, the issue of discrimination against Muslims is one faced by many teachers and students in the United States. It is an issue of great importance in New York City, where it is estimated that more than 600,000 Muslims live and work. Since 9/11, the number of Muslims living in the United States has doubled, and this issue of religious discrimination against Muslims is one that is directly related to the U.S. Constitution and one's rights to free exercise of religion and speech.

This social studies teacher wanted his students to learn more about Islam as a religion, to better understand the difference between religious practice and fanaticism, to develop their own research questions about Islam, to consider discrimination against Muslims in relation to the U.S. Constitution, to better understand the process through which young people get indoctrinated into fanatical Islamic groups, and to come up with ways to further educate the school community and prevent further discrimination and violence against Muslims.

Two primary texts the teacher selected for the read-and-revisit unit were the *New York Times* bestsellers *Three Cups of Tea: One Man's Mission to Promote Peace One School at a Time*, written by Greg Mortenson and David Oliver Relin (2007), and *Infidel*, written by Ayaan Hirsi Ali (2007). Because this teacher was my graduate student at the time, his unit included a short commentary that I published in the National Council of Teachers of English (NCTE) publication *English Journal* titled "Teaching in the Days after September 11, 2001" (Darvin, 2002). At the conclusion of the unit, several students in the class chose to continue reading further on this topic in their social studies book clubs and self-selected *Stones into Schools: Promoting Peace with Books, Not Bombs, in Afghanistan and Pakistan*, Greg Mortenson's (2009) sequel to *Three Cups of Tea*.

The Prereading CPVs and CPV Activities

To introduce the Islam read-and-revisit unit, the teacher began by presenting the class with two CPVs to answer in writing for homework. He used these CPVs as a way to help uncover his students' initial thoughts and opinions on the topics surrounding discrimination against Muslims and to establish a baseline from which to measure growth and the acquisition of new knowledge, after students were exposed to the texts, CPV activities, and class discussions.

The first prereading CPV read as follows:

You lost a family member in the terrorist bombing of the World Trade Center on September 11, 2001. You receive a letter telling you that a new mosque is scheduled to be erected a block away from Ground Zero next year, but the landowner wants to take your opinion and those of other family members who lost loved ones on 9/11 into consideration before finalizing his plans and beginning construction. What would you say and/or do, and why?

The second prereading CPV read as follows:

You have volunteered, with your parents' permission, to host an exchange student from another country in your family's home for 3 months during your senior year of high school. The exchange student will live in your home and attend your high school. You will be spending a lot of time with him or her. You receive a letter from the school explaining that there is a Muslim exchange student from Afghanistan who is interested in coming, but he or she can do so only if you and your parents agree to serve as host family. What would you say and/or do, and why?

When the students returned to class the next day with their CPV responses, the teacher began by putting students into small groups to share and discuss their written responses verbally with one another. He then asked them to come up with a list of similarities and differences between the two situations presented in the prereading CPVs. The teacher chose to include a compare/contrast aspect in the assignment because he thought this would enable students to more easily identify the various subtleties of the CPVs' prompts, and that comparing and contrasting the CPV situations would give them greater opportunities to evaluate both from multiple perspectives. After doing so in small groups, students then shared their lists with the whole class and created master lists of similarities and differences that included the following:

Similarities

- Both CPVs deal with situations involving Muslims.
- In both situations, the person in the CPV is being asked to respond to a letter.
- Both CPVs have more than one side to consider when responding.
- In both situations, the letter is asking for an opinion and agreement or disagreement with something.
- Both CPVs relate to discrimination against Muslims.
- In both CPVs, the respondent has to consider the feelings and opinions of his or her family members.

Differences

- In the first CPV, the person lost a family member in 9/11, and in the second, he or she didn't.
- The first CPV deals with the rights of many people to practice their religion, but the second one is only talking about one person's rights to an education.
- The first CPV involves building a mosque, which is a public place of worship. The second one involves one student's education.
- The first CPV is about adult Muslims, and the second is related to a kid (teenager).
- The first CPV is more political than the second because it involves 9/11 and Ground Zero. The second CPV is more personal than the first because it deals more with family, cultural, and school issues.

After creating these lists of similarities and differences, many students also shared excerpts from their written responses with the class, both in their small groups and whole-class discussion.

For CPV 1, the mosque CPV, some of the excerpts included the following:

Of all of the places to build a mosque, why put it near Ground Zero? I mean, that's just like throwing it in people's faces whose family members died in 9/11. I think it is fine to build a mosque. I mean, it's New York City, but near Ground Zero is not an appropriate place to put one.

I don't think they should build a mosque there because it will just get bombed or burned down by angry families from 9/11.

I would tell them not to build the mosque there because Muslims are mostly terrorists, and then they will be right next door to blow up the new World Trade Center once it's rebuilt.

I don't think they should build the mosque there because the Muslim men and women don't go to the mosque together. The women can't even go to the mosque with their husbands or sons, so they should not build it.

For CPV 2, the exchange student CPV, excerpts included the following:

I wouldn't mind if a Muslim kid came to stay with me, but I know my father wouldn't want them to come because he calls them bad names like towel head and A-Rab, so I would have to respect my dad's house and say, no, I'm sorry.

I wouldn't want a Muslim kid to come live with us. It's not because of us, though. It's because of them. I just don't think that he would fit in or be comfortable. It's probably better for him if he stays with his own kind so they know what he can eat, and when he has to pray and stuff.

I would want the Afghani kid to just come. Why not?

I would tell the people, "no thank you." We don't want to host that kid, but maybe if they have one from Italy, they could send her instead. My family is Italian, and we could speak Italian to her and take her to Little Italy.

My mom wouldn't want that kid to come stay with us because she is afraid of terrorists and bad people like that. She would only feel comfortable hosting a Jewish student. We have relatives in Israel who fight with the Muslims all the time, so that wouldn't be a good idea for a Jewish family.

The Texts and During-Reading Activities

After sharing their initial responses and creating their lists of similarities and differences, students began reading their self-selected texts, either *Three Cups of Tea* or *Infidel*. They were given a choice between the two books; prior to the students' making their selections, the teacher did what he termed a book "infomercial" on each one, briefly summarizing the books, providing information about the authors, and sharing the reviews, awards, and accolades the books had received (Gallagher, 2003). He passed several copies of the books around the class so students could view their cover designs, photographic inserts, and see firsthand that the length of both books was rather long, approximately 350 pages.

Not surprisingly, the majority of the female students chose to read *Infidel*, the true story of Hirsi Ali, a Muslim woman who survived, despite many extraordinary challenges, including civil war, beatings, female mutilation, escape from an arranged marriage, and other injustices. She was granted asylum in the Netherlands, where she earned a college degree and later fought for Muslim women's rights and the reform of Islam as a member of the Dutch Parliament. Under constant threat by Muslim extremists, and disowned by her father, family, and clan, Ali refused to stop fighting for her beliefs.

The female students were immediately intrigued by the story of a female freedom fighter who was born in Mogadishu and traveled to Saudi Arabia, Ethiopia, Kenya, and the Netherlands, fighting for her own rights and those of Muslim women everywhere. They wanted to know how she was able to be so courageous and go against the strong beliefs of so many men. They told their teacher that they wanted to read this book because "for once, there is a female hero in the story."

Conversely, most male students chose to read *Three Cups of Tea*, a book with an American male protagonist, who was also a champion of Muslim women's right to education. In 1993, mountain climber Greg Mortenson attempted to climb K2 in Pakistan and failed in his attempt, nearly killing himself in the process. The mountaineer was so moved by the kindness of the Pakistani people who saved his life and nursed him back to health that he promised to return to their remote mountain village to build a school. *Three Cups of Tea* is the story of how Mortenson later returned and fulfilled that promise by building not one, but 55 schools for girls in that region over the next 10 years. When asked why they chose this book over *Infidel*, several of the boys indicated that the quote on the back cover was the true reason for their selection. The quote reads, "The astonishing, uplifting story of a real-life Indiana Jones and his remarkable humanitarian campaign in the Taliban's Backyard."

While reading the texts, students engaged in many literacy activities, several of which included the use of shorter texts that related to the overarching themes of the unit and class novels. For example, at the time that students were studying this topic, there was a real controversy brewing about a proposed mosque and Islamic cultural center being built near Ground Zero in Manhattan. The teacher, in an effort to incorporate authentic current events that could be viewed from multiple perspectives into the unit, had students read several newspaper articles about the real "Park51" debate, including an article that the *New York Times* published in 2010 titled "Islamic Center Exposes Mixed Feelings Locally," by Paul Vitello.

The students read a total of six current events articles on the proposed mosque near Ground Zero debate, some in favor and others opposed. Students discussed various viewpoints presented in the articles, and the teacher then added some primary source document analysis to the debate by having students review those portions of the U.S. Constitution that deal with the rights to freedom of religion and speech. According to the teacher, it was fascinating to see how students were able to make text-to-self, text-to-world, and text-to-text connections and to operationalize the Constitution through the lens of a controversial current event.

In addition to the current events–related readings and discussions, students engaged in situated performances of the two teacher-generated prereading CPVs, as well as several new ones that they produced themselves. The teacher combined the Create and Exchange stage (Stage 2) with the Situated Performance stage (Stage 3) in such a way that students created, exchanged, and performed CPVs that they generated from their readings and class discussions.

For example, while reading *Three Cups of Tea*, several of the male students became intrigued with trying to understand exactly how and why the Taliban recruits young children, brainwashes them into committing terrible acts of violence against innocent people, and even encourages and facilitates acts of suicide. They compared this modern-day phenomena to the ways in which Adolf Hitler indoctrinated the Hitler Youth, using Nazi propaganda, and convinced them to commit acts of torture and murder against European Jews during World War II in the 1940s. This particular group of male students created a CPV situated performance in which they demonstrated some of the brainwashing techniques used by the Taliban on its young, poor, starving recruits.

A second group of female students who were reading *Infidel* was interested in revealing to their classmates some of the terrible injustices that young Muslim women their age face every day in countries such as Saudi Arabia and Pakistan. They created a CPV situated performance that showcased several of these injustices, including a young woman being forced to dress in a full-body burqa or chador in an oppressively hot climate, denied the right to attend school, beaten by her father regularly, and forced to marry an older man whom she doesn't know or love in an arranged marriage. Students were careful to preface their situated performance by explaining to their classmates, through the use of a narrator, that if a woman *chooses* to wear a burqa or to allow her family to select her husband, that is a cultural choice, rather than an oppressive act that violates her freedoms and rights as a human being.

Postreading and Extended Read-and-Revisit Activities

At the conclusion of the unit, students engaged in several postreading read-and-revisit activities that encouraged them to reflect on changes in their thinking about Islam and the acquisition of new knowledge throughout the unit. They were instructed to look back at their earlier responses to the mosque and exchange-student CPVs and reflect on specific changes in their thinking and why these changes occurred. Additionally, individual groups of students were asked to share what they had learned about subtopics they had researched with the rest of the class through situated performances and technology-enhanced oral presentations.

One group, for example, chose to focus their final situated performance and presentation on the significance of drinking tea in Pakistani society. In Mortenson's book, Haji Ali, the Korphe Village Chief in Pakistan, tells Mortenson that in Afghanistan and Pakistan, men drink three cups of tea to do business. He says that for the first cup, you are a stranger, the second a friend, and the third, you join our family, and for family we are prepared to die. The students explained how at the beginning of the unit they did not understand this kind of cultural thinking. As

Americans, they had difficulty comprehending why Mortenson's promise to build a school meant so much to the people of the village, and how in Pakistani Muslim society a person's word still carries so much weight. As part of their presentation, students prepared tea for the class and taught them about ways they can help support the construction of schools in that region of the world. They showed them the website Pennies for Peace, an organization designed for schoolchildren to raise money for education and literacy in the Middle East, and encouraged them to get involved in a fundraising project they were spearheading.

A second group of students focused their read-and-revisit situated performance and presentation specifically on the mosque CPV and changes in their thinking as a result of the unit. They explained that they now believed that the mosque could be built near Ground Zero, as long as it was done in such a way that it was sensitive to the family members of the 9/11 victims. In their situated performance, they emphasized educating people to differentiate between mainstream Islam and fanatical Islamic groups as being vital to the creation of the mosque, particularly in that delicate location. In their skit, the Muslim leaders of the mosque invited family members of 9/11 victims to attend a memorial ceremony that remembered the 9/11 victims and paid tribute to them. They also emphasized that the mosque should serve as a cultural center that would have lectures, films, and workshops that would teach people in the community about Islam in positive ways. They believed strongly as a result of this unit of study that the rights of Muslims in America must be protected under the U.S. Constitution

A third group of students focused their read-and-revisit situated performance and presentation specifically on the exchange-student CPV. Several students in the group that had originally written about themselves or their parents not wanting to house a Muslim student from Afghanistan in their homes changed their thinking as a result of the unit. Their situated performance centered on a positive cultural exchange between an American high school student and an Afghani exchange student. In their skit, the young Afghani woman teaches her American female host about her Muslim clothing in different contexts: clothing for everyday wear, inside and outside the house, and clothing required in specifically religious contexts. At the conclusion of the skit, the American high school student teaches what she has learned about her Afghani friend's culture with her mother, thus reducing her mom's ignorance about and possible discomfort with their exchange student's form of dress. The students explained that they wanted to address the fact that their parents are often afraid of things that they do not understand or things with which they are unfamiliar and how they, as younger people, can help by being catalysts for their parents to change their thinking.

Finally, students, as part of their read-and-revisit situated performances and presentations, were encouraged to engage in continued, extended projects after completion of the unit and to share aspects of what they had learned with the rest of their schoolmates, outside of their own classroom. To do so, students did several things, including watching Hirsi Ali and Theo van Gogh's film *Submission: Part I* after school and leading a postviewing conversation about the film; reading and discussing articles that Ali posted on the website of the American Enterprise Institute for Public Policy Research, a Washington, D.C., think tank; reading *Stones into Schools: Promoting Peace with Books, Not Bombs, in Afghanistan and Pakistan* as a book club selection, and encouraging other students schoolwide to purchase the book via Amazon, where up to 7% of all their book and other purchases can go to the Central Asia Institute and be sent to a girls' education scholarship fund in Afghanistan and Pakistan; writing book reviews of Ali's and Mortenson's books and posting them on education blogs and booksellers' websites (e.g., Amazon, Barnes & Noble, Goodreads) to bring awareness to these books and the causes about which they educate the public; and raising money with a car wash and bake sale to donate to Pennies for Peace, an organization that is committed to making a difference in Afghani and Pakistani students' lives, one penny and one pencil at a time.

The social studies teacher who designed this read-and-revisit unit on Islam was pleased with the tremendous growth in his students' thinking, particularly about an issue that is culturally and politically sensitive, timely, and complex. He reflected on the unit's success as follows:

I wanted my students to better understand Islam as a religion, recognize the differences between religious practice and fanaticism, consider discrimination against Muslims in relation to the United States Constitution, gain understanding of the processes by which young people get indoctrinated into fanatical religious groups, and design and implement ways to further educate their school community and prevent further discrimination and violence against Muslims. I believe that the use of CPVs and situated performances in this read-and-revisit unit made these goals easier to attain and provided my students with ample opportunities to discuss, question, and interact with the material in ways that promoted critical literacy and fostered growth and reflection. I am particularly pleased that students were so motivated that they chose to continue their efforts beyond the classroom walls, the hallmark of critical literacy at its best.

In addition to encompassing many of the aspects of critical literacy discussed in earlier chapters of this book, this unit also exemplifies many aspects of the CCSS.

ELEVENTH-GRADE CPV READ-AND-REVISIT ACTIVITIES AND LINKS TO THE CCSS

In order to be successful with this read-and-revisit unit, students had to display the capacities of the literate individual to which the CCSS refer in their portrait of students who are college and career ready in reading, writing, speaking, listening, and language. They were encouraged to demonstrate independence; build content knowledge; respond to the varying demands of audience, task, purpose, and discipline; comprehend as well as critique; value evidence; employ technology capably;

and come to understand other perspectives and cultures. The last capacity regarding the development of greater cultural understanding is one that enables students to communicate more effectively with people of varied backgrounds, and in the case of this particular school, this unit might have helped to prevent discrimination and violence against Muslims. Figure 5.3 depicts some of the specific links between this unit and the CCSS.

Figure 5.3. 11th-Grade Read-and-Revisit CPV Unit and Links to the CCSS

Understanding Islam	11th Grade	Read-and-Revisit CPV Unit and Links to the CCSS
Some of the Student Performance Indicators/Objectives Addressed in the CPV Unit	*CCSS Number*	*Corresponding Common Core State Standard(s) (CCSS)*
Students read sections of the U.S. Constitution and determined whether preventing Muslims from building a mosque near Ground Zero is a violation of their freedoms to practice their religion and free speech.	RL.8	Delineate and evaluate the reasoning in seminal U.S. texts, including the application of constitutional principles and use of legal reasoning and the premises, purposes, and arguments in works of public advocacy.
When creating their situated performances to teach the class about their Islam subtopics, students made many decisions regarding technique, details, and sequences.	W.3	Write narratives to develop real or imagined experiences or events using effective technique, well-chosen details, and well-structured event sequences.
Students generated questions they had about Islam and narrowed their inquiries to focus on and research particular aspects of the religion with which they had questions, wanting to deepen their understanding. They combined what they learned from various sources into their CPV situated performances and oral presentations.	W.7	Conduct short as well as more sustained research projects to answer a question (including a self-generated question) or solve a problem; narrow or broaden the inquiry when appropriate; synthesize multiple sources on the subject, demonstrating understanding of the subject under investigation.
In their oral presentations and extended projects, students used PowerPoint, YouTube videos, and websites to enhance the audience's understanding and to create curiosity.	SL.5	Make strategic use of digital media in presentations to enhance understanding of findings, reasoning, and evidence and to add interest.

Overall, this read-and-revisit CPV unit exemplifies the CCSS for English, language arts, and literacy being applied in history/social studies. This social studies teacher asked his students to read, write, discuss, and listen to discipline-specific content and to consciously reflect on changes in their thinking over time, as they acquired new knowledge. Most important, the inquiries that students began in class extended beyond the confines of their social studies course and expanded into their school and larger community, hallmarks of critical literacy at its very best and most effective.

CLOSING THOUGHTS ON STAGE 4 OF CPV IMPLEMENTATION

Of all of the stages of CPV implementation, Stage 4 is the most effective in allowing you to track and evaluate changes in your students' thinking and knowledge base over time. When revisiting CPV prompts, students have opportunities to highlight changes in their thinking and improvements in their problem-solving abilities as a result of being exposed to key course texts, class discussions, situated performances, and a variety of literacy tasks that are part of CPV curricular units. I encourage you to experiment with Stage 4 and allow your students to engage in both short-term and long-term read-and-revisit units. Doing so will not only benefit your students but also enable you to better evaluate the impact that particular course texts have on your students and inform your decisions on whether to continue using these texts or replace them with more effective ones.

CHAPTER 6

Conclusion

In the Introduction to this book, I discussed an uncomfortable personal experience that I had 23 years ago, as a novice English teacher working with Melville's *Billy Budd, Sailor*, when one of my students raised his hand and asked if Melville was gay.

If that same situation were to occur in my classroom today, I would have a completely different reaction and response from what I had then. Rather than shying away from a conversation about an author's sexual identity and how it might have influenced his writing and character development, I would seize the question as an opportunity and entry point into critical dialogue and literacy development for my students. In fact, in anticipation of this controversial topic being brought up, I would have already designed engaging CPV activities around *Billy Budd, Sailor* and the theme of homosexuality. These CPV activities would provide my students with ample opportunities to think critically, discuss, read, write, engage in situated performances, and revisit their previously held opinions with regard to various aspects of homosexuality, including how society viewed it historically versus presently and its possible impacts on an author's writing and perspective.

HOW CPVS HAVE IMPROVED MY TEACHING

CPVs have helped to significantly alter my approach to teaching and learning because they have given me a pedagogical framework with which to help students develop critical literacy around culturally and politically sensitive issues. They have provided me with ways to both document and assess my students' growth and learning about important social issues, while concurrently addressing and moving beyond the CCSS and other curricular mandates and standards. Most important, however, CPVs have enabled me to let go of teaching practices that value the coverage of material and move into the kind of teaching that I believe helps make my students more critical consumers of information and better prepared citizens of their classrooms, schools, and communities.

Happily, I am not the only educator who has embraced CPVs as a pedagogical approach that facilitates critical thinking and literacy development. Teachers whose work has been featured throughout this book and others who have been using the CPV model in their secondary classrooms have also experienced positive outcomes after using CPVs to foster critical literacy development among their students. As part of my ongoing research and scholarship on secondary students' and teachers' experiences with CPVs, I have asked many teachers to document and reflect on their experiences. Their responses demonstrate how and why CPVs are a powerful pedagogical tool in developing critical literacy.

THREE KEY LEARNING GAINS REPORTED BY TEACHERS USING CPVS

An informal analysis of more than 200 teacher reflections on using CPVs in their secondary classrooms reveals three major areas in which teachers believe CPVs help promote critical literacy development. The first is an increase in student motivation and engagement. The second is an increase in the complex communication skills exhibited by students. The third is that teachers themselves feel empowered by CPVs to teach for social justice and values clarification. Many of the teacher reflections also indicate that CPVs helped them to better realize the CCSS unobtrusively in their courses.

Increasing Student Motivation and Engagement

Teachers who use CPV activities with their students strongly believe that it is a pedagogical model that enhances student motivation and engagement, a critical goal with adolescent learners in particular.

Here is a comment from one English teacher:

One of the greatest challenges when teaching high school students is getting them interested enough in the material that they want to stay awake and read and write about it. Many of the texts that we use at this level are boring to students, but the CPV activities get at the "juicy stuff" in the reading material and help provide motivation for my students to want to sit up and talk about it and then read, write, and do research.

Another English teacher stated the following:

CPV activities have been very helpful in reducing the classroom-management issues in my classes. I've learned that the majority of behavioral problems at this level stem from students' boredom and lack of engagement with the material. Once you provide a hook in the lesson that is engaging and give students interesting topics to dialogue and write about, the discipline problems decrease and you are able to get to the critical literacy development that we all strive for as English teachers.

A teacher of social studies addressed the motivational aspects of CPVs in her comments:

Most kids find history to be really boring and inaccessible. They think that it's all about memorizing facts about dead guys and remembering dates and events, with little connection to themselves and their own lives. CPVs, because of their thematic nature, have allowed me to motivate my students to want to learn about social studies. Kids like to talk about controversial social issues, and with CPVs, it's easy for me to engage my students in respectful, critical dialogue around a culturally or politically charged issue, while still teaching them the content of history and how the past relates to the present and future. I am glad to have pedagogical tools at my disposal that motivate students to want to talk about history and view historical events and issues through multiple perspectives.

A middle school social studies teacher agreed:

The first and most important aspect of any lesson with adolescent learners is engagement. When my students create and exchange their own CPVs and enact situated performances, they are such active participants in their own learning. I find that they love the CPV activities and can't wait to perform in front of their peers and critically analyze their own performances and those of their classmates. Since I started using CPV activities in my classes, I've noticed that the participation of my students has greatly increased, especially with my special education students. I like the fact that I, as the teacher, take on more of a facilitator role, while the students become more active and engaged with the text.

Along similar lines, many of the teacher reflections discuss their satisfaction with the four stages of CPV implementation as a gradual release model in which students take on more and more responsibility for their literacy learning over the course of the school year. The teacher reflections reveal that this model is empowering to students and authentically mirrors the way people engage with text in the real world as they problem-pose and problem-solve. In summation, the secondary teachers who employ CPV activities believe that they increase student engagement and motivation, two areas that are critical to teaching and learning at this level.

Enhancing Complex Communication Skills

A second theme that emerged in the teacher reflections relates to the ways in which teachers believe that CPVs enhance students' complex communication skills. One middle school ELA teacher described it this way:

One of the best things about CPVs is the fact that they enable students to practice and hone their listening and speaking skills, not just their reading and writing. Although the ELA standards always list reading, writing, speaking, and listening as the four modes of communication, it is rare that we work on speaking and listening skills in ELA classes. If we do, it is at very low levels. CPVs give me a platform by which to work on my students' speaking and listening skills at a very high level. Since we began using situated performances in my classes, I've noticed a great improvement in my students' speaking and listening skills. They want to be understood and to understand one another. It's very refreshing.

And a teacher of high school social studies reported the following:

Since the advent of using CPVs in my classes, the students' communication skills during group-work have improved dramatically. The students don't laugh at each other or tease each other during class discussions, and I find they are getting better at not interrupting and listening to one another's opinions critically. The other day, during a small-group CPV discussion, I overheard one of my students say to another group member, "We haven't heard from you yet. What do you think about this?" I was really surprised to hear my students communicating so effectively.

Similarly, a high school English teacher had these comments:

One of the most difficult and complex aspects of communication, even for adults, involves how to express your opinions to others who have different or opposing views in ways that are appropriate and courteous. I think that CPVs are really helpful in teaching students how to listen to each other's opinions, critically analyze them, and share in conversations that open up their minds and thinking to possibilities that may have never occurred to them.

A middle school social studies teacher pointed out the following:

Adolescence is a time when students are learning how to communicate in more complex ways than when they were young children. They are forming their identities and learning about who they are in the world and what they believe. They are learning how to articulate their thoughts and feelings to others. The CPV model gives students a safe space to talk, read, and write about issues that have an impact on their development as people and critical thinkers. I am thankful that my students can practice their higher-level communication skills in my classroom, so that any mistakes they make along the way can serve as lessons for what not to do or say in the real world.

Teaching for Social Justice and Values Clarification

The final and most powerful theme that became apparent in nearly all the teacher reflections analyzed involved the ways in which CPVs enable teachers to promote social justice and values clarification in their secondary classrooms. These two terms are a bit problematic in that they mean many different things to different people, but for the purposes they are being used here, it is not necessary or even possible to define them specifically because they emerged naturally from the teachers' own reflections and were not introduced to them or defined for them prior to their writing their reflections.

With regard to teaching for social justice, teachers frequently referred to the Freirian ideal that has been discussed throughout this volume in relation to using critical literacy to actually *do something* positive to benefit members of an oppressed, misunderstood, or disenfranchised group in the students' classroom, school, or larger community. As mentioned in the Introduction, my view of teaching for social justice involves attempting to right some kind of wrong or teach in ways that reveal social injustices to students and invite them to problem-solve and create possible solutions to help alleviate these injustices. Teaching for social justice can involve a relatively small issue, such as getting a group of kids to stop bullying an individual student in the class, or larger issues, such as creating a schoolwide mental wellness program or helping fight homelessness in the community.

With regard to the term "values clarification," or what one teacher termed "teaching my students how to be good citizens" and another dubbed "making my students active and informed members of a democratic society," teachers must be careful not to cross the line and advocate morals or ethics to their impressionable adolescent students. The goals of the CPV model are similar to the values clarification strategies of the 1970s (Simon, Howe, & Kirschenbaum, 1978) discussed earlier in this book: to engage students in practical experiences; make them aware of their own feelings, ideas, and beliefs; and help them to make conscious and deliberate choices and decisions *based on their own value systems*. This does not equate to telling students the right and wrong ways to think and act, but rather to making them more aware of their own thoughts and actions so they might modify them accordingly, based on their own developing value systems.

One ELA teacher encapsulated this concept in her comments:

CPVs provide a lens through which my students can see and elucidate their own views about controversial topics, as well as those of their classmates. When using the Read and Revisit stage of CPVs, in particular, I am able to see the changes in their thinking over time and how interacting with the text and dialoging with their classmates influences them in positive and sometimes negative ways. I don't tell them what I think is right or lead them down particular paths. CPVs provide opportunities for them to do these things on their own, indications that they are not only increasing their knowledge of the subject matter at hand, but concurrently clarifying their own belief systems and ideals.

A teacher of high school social studies maintains the following:

A big part of how I view my role as a social studies teacher is to teach for social justice and create students who will be active and informed citizens of a global, democratic society. I want my students to be educated consumers of information, particularly that which comes to them from the television, media, and Internet sources. More than any other pedagogical strategies I've used with my students,

I believe that CPVs provide my students with ways to consider information from multiple perspectives and look at whose voices are heard and whose are silenced with regard to pivotal historical and social issues.

Another secondary history teacher made the following argument:

I know that we are supposed to stick to teaching the "content" of social studies, but I believe that I would be remiss in my teaching of social studies if I did not try to at least teach my students to be good citizens in a general sense. I never try to push my cultural views or political preferences onto my students, but I do try to present information to them that teaches them right from wrong, at least implicitly or subliminally. CPVs are really helpful in getting my students to reflect on their own beliefs and, hopefully, improve upon them over time. I also like the action component of CPVs because what good is all this talk about teaching for social justice if students never do anything positive in their schools and communities? I think CPVs have given me the motivation to extend many of my students' inquiries beyond the classroom. This is real teaching for social justice in my view.

BEYOND THE CCSS

Throughout this book, much attention has been paid to the CCSS and the multitude of ways in which CPV curricular units address the CCSS and exemplify what good CCSS-based units might entail. As discussed previously, CPV units mirror all of the key design considerations of the CCSS, the specific CCSS at various grade levels and disciplines, as well as the qualities desired by the CCSS authors in their portrait of "Students Who are College and Career Ready in Reading, Writing, Speaking, Listening and Language."

One of the greatest strengths of the CPV model is that it helps to fill the pedagogical void that is intentionally created by the CCSS's key design consideration, "A focus on results rather than means." The CCSS deliberately claim that "the Standards leave room for teachers, curriculum developers, and states to determine how [those] goals should be reached and what additional topics should be addressed."

The CCSS are very careful not to mandate, recommend, or advocate particular writing processes, metacognitive strategies, or literacy programs. The CPV model, as demonstrated throughout this book and its varied curricular examples, provides teachers with several helpful pedagogical methods and tools to help them achieve the CCSS in their classrooms, without being scripted.

In addition to all of the ways that CPV activities embody the CCSS, it is important to recognize the ways in which the CPV model moves *beyond* the CCSS to address matters that cannot be adequately described or required by the CCSS and other standards and curricular mandates. Standards such as the CCSS, no matter how carefully constructed and detailed, cannot possibly speak to higher societal goals, such as teaching and learning for values clarification and social justice. As evidenced by the excerpts from the teacher reflections, these goals represent qualities desired by secondary teachers for something that the CCSS, if they could or dared, might term "Students Who are Democracy, Real Life, and World Ready in Their Reading, Writing, Speaking, Listening, and Language." In other words, the CPV model thoroughly speaks to the CCSS, but it also moves beyond them in the empowering ways that it positions teachers and students with regard to their critical literacy development.

Whereas the CCSS, for example, speak about a desired portrait of students who "come to understand other perspectives and cultures," what does a student's *understanding* of a perspective or culture actually look like in the real world? Is it enough for students to simply *understand* another perspective or culture, or is there an implicit, more important expectation that this new cultural understanding should then lead to positive change in a learner's subsequent actions as she or he relates to a real or imagined problem or conflict? In this example, the CPV model moves beyond the CCSS's goal of simply *understanding* another perspective or culture and extends into the Freirian ideal of a learner's responsibility to use this new knowledge of perspective and culture to foster positive change in his or her classroom, school, or community.

The CCSS, like all standards, propose a single set of learning goals *for all students*. As you have seen in the many examples provided in this book, CPVs are open-ended enough to respond to specific situations that students face in their particular school and community contexts. In addition to being flexible in terms of the situations to which they can respond, CPVs are useful in differentiating instruction, so that all students are able to engage fully with challenging questions, even if they need support in doing so. This contrasts with the unfortunate trend being seen in many schools today in which students in need of academic support are given very basic worksheets and scripted curricula that don't allow for analytical thought, problem solving, critical reading, or other forms of powerful literacy (Finn, 2009).

Many of the best and most important lessons that students learn as a result of engaging with the kinds of CPV units that were featured in this book cannot be adequately measured by the CCSS because they are, quite frankly, beyond the scope of things that standards such as the CCSS could ever hope to address or measure. Secondary teachers, as evidenced in their previous reflections, want their students to be and do all of the wonderful things that the CCSS describe, *and then some*. By employing the CPV model in their classrooms, secondary teachers can achieve all the goals of the CCSS with their students, while also providing them with priceless opportunities to move beyond the CCSS. Moving beyond the CCSS includes critical literacy development that encourages students to reflect on and clarify their own values; analyze, discuss, problem-pose, and problem-solve around pivotal culturally and politically sensitive issues; and take actions that lead to greater social awareness and social justice.

Directory of CPVs by Grade Level, Subject, and Topic/Tough Issue

Chapter & Page Number(s)	Grade Level	Subject	Topic
Intro., p. 6	8th grade	U.S. history	Slavery
Ch. 1, pp. 17–19	7th grade	Language arts	Bullying
Ch. 1, p. 21	Middle school	Language arts	Substance abuse
Ch. 1, p. 22	High school	Language arts	Prescription drug abuse
Ch. 1, p. 24	12th grade	Participation in government	September 11, 2001
Ch. 1, p. 25	8th grade	Language arts	Mob violence
Ch. 2, p. 38	6th grade	Social studies	Improving group work
Ch. 2, p. 39	7th grade	Home & careers	Kitchen safety
Ch. 2, p.43	12th Grade	English	Suicide
Ch. 2, pp. 44–45	11th Grade	U.S. history	The Holocaust
Ch. 3, pp. 52–53	7th Grade	Language arts	Overcoming Adversity:Divorce, smoking, and moving
Ch. 3, p. 58	7th Grade	Language arts	Mental illness: Depression and self-mutilation

(continued)

Appendix (continued)

Chapter & Page Number(s)	Grade Level	Subject	Topic
Ch. 3, p. 68	10th and 11th grade	Global studies and U.S. history	Child soldiers, the Vietnam War, Bosnia, and the American Civil War
Ch. 4, pp. 77–85	9th grade	English	Interracial dating, racial pride, racial profiling, and police brutality
Ch. 4, pp. 85–94	12th grade	Participation in government	Homelessness in America
Ch. 5, p. 100	8th grade	Language arts	Child abuse
Ch. 5, pp. 104–105	8th grade	Language arts	Date rape and sexual assault
Ch. 5, p. 114	11th grade	U.S. history	Understanding Islam and preventing discrimination

Please note that the page numbers above apply only to print versions of the book. Ebook readers are encouraged to use the search tool to find particular CPVs and tough issues in the text.

References

Adams, M., Bell, L. A., & Griffin, P. (Eds.). (2007). *Teaching for diversity and social justice.* New York, NY: Routledge.

Alfieri, L., Brooks, P. J., Aldrich, N. J., & Tenenbaum, H. R. (2011). Does discovery-based instruction enhance learning? *Journal of Educational Psychology, 103*(1), 1.

Ali, A. H. (2007). *Infidel.* New York, NY: Free Press.

Anderson, L. H. (1999). *Speak.* New York, NY: Square Fish.

Apple, M. W. (2014). *Official knowledge: Democratic education in a conservative age.* New York, NY: Routledge.

Barton, K. C., & Levstik, L. S. (2003). Why don't more history teachers engage students in interpretation? *Special Education, 67*(6), 358–361.

Beah, I. (2008). *A long way gone: Memoirs of a boy soldier.* New York, NY: Sarah Crichton Books.

Bell, L. A. (2010). *Storytelling for social justice: Connecting narrative and the arts in antiracist teaching.* New York, NY: Routledge.

Ben-Peretz, M. (2001). The impossible role of teacher educators in a changing world. *Journal of Teacher Education, 52*(48), 48–56.

Bolnick, J. P., & Bolnick, S. T. (2001). *Living at the edge of the world: How I survived in the tunnels of Grand Central Station.* New York, NY: St. Martin's Griffin.

Christensen, L. (2000). *Reading, writing and rising up: Teaching about social justice and the power of the written word.* Milwaukee, WI: Rethinking Schools.

Clandinin, D. J. (2013). Chapter 4: Personal practical knowledge: A study of teachers' classroom images. In C. J. Craig, P. C. Meijer, & J. Broeckmans (Eds.), *From teacher thinking to teachers and teaching: The evolution of a research community* (pp. 67–95). *(Advances in Research on Teaching, Volume 19).* Bingley, West Yorkshire, United Kingdom: Emerald Group Publishing Limited.

Cochran-Smith, M. (2005). The new teacher education: For better or for worse? *Educational Researcher, 34*(7), 3–17.

Connelly, F. M., & Clandinin, D. J. (1988). *Teachers as curriculum planners: Narratives of experience.* New York, NY: Teachers College Press.

Copeland, M. (2010). *Socratic circles: Fostering critical and creative thinking in middle and high school.* Portland, ME: Stenhouse.

Craig, C. J. (2007). Story constellations: A narrative approach to contextualizing teachers' knowledge of school reform. *Teaching and Teacher Education, 23*(2), 173–188.

Craig, C. J., & Ross, V. (2008). Cultivating the image of teachers as curriculum makers. In F. M. Connelly, M. F. He, & J. I. Phillion (Eds.), *The SAGE handbook of curriculum and instruction* (pp. 282–305). Thousand Oaks, CA: Sage Publications.

Daniels, H., & Zemelman, S. (2014). *Subjects matter: Every teacher's guide to content-area reading* (2nd ed.). Portsmouth, NH: Heinemann.

Darvin, J. (2002). Teaching in the days after September 11, 2001. *English Journal, 91*(4), 18–19.

Darvin, J. (2009). Cultural and political vignettes in the English classroom: Problem-posing, problem-solving, and the imagination. *English Journal, 92*(2), 55–60.

Darvin, J. (2010). Using cultural and political vignettes to explore justice issues in teacher education courses. In C. Rhodes & L. Wolf (Eds.), *Social justice and education: Navigating stormy waters.* East Rockaway, NY: Cummings & Hathaway Publishers.

Darvin, J. (2011a) I don't feel comfortable reading those books in my classroom: A qualitative study of the impact of cultural and political vignettes in a teacher education course. *The Teacher Educator, 46*(4), 274–298.

Darvin, J. (2011b). I would rather feel uncomfortable in an education class than at the school where I teach: Cultural and political vignettes as a pedagogical approach in teacher education. In A. Cohan & A. Honigsfeld (Eds.), *Breaking the mold of pre-service and in-service teacher education* (pp. 15–23). Lantham, MD: R & L Education.

Darvin, J. (2011c). Situated performances in a graduate teacher education course: An inquiry into the impact of cultural and political vignettes (CPVs). *Teachers and Teaching: Theory and Practice, 17*(3), 345–364.

Darvin, J. (2011d). Teaching critical literacy using cultural and political vignettes. *Critical Education, 2*(6). Retrieved from http://m1.cust.educ.ubc.ca/journal/index.php/criticaled/article/view/155

Darvin, J. (2012). Supporting teachers with professional development that reflects how the teacing profession is changing. *Principal*, March/April issue.

Downy, A. L. (2005). The transformative power of drama: Bringing literature and social justice to life. *English Journal, 95*(1), 33–38.

Eisner, E. (1988). Foreword. In F. M. Connelly & D. J. Clandinin (Eds.), *Teachers as curriculum planners: Narratives of experience.* New York, NY: Teachers College Press.

Eitington, J. E. (1996). *Winning ways to involve people in learning.* Houston, TX: Gulf Publishing Co.

Fang, Z., Lamme, L. L., & Pringle, R. M. (2010). *Language and literacy in inquiry-based science classrooms, grades 3–8.* Thousand Oaks, CA: Sage.

Filipovic, Z. (1994). *Zlata's diary: A child's life in Sarajevo.* New York, NY: Viking.

Finders, M., & Rose, S. (1999). If I were the teacher: Situated performances as pedagogical tools for teacher preparation. *English Education, 31*(3), 205–222.

Finn, P. J. (2009). *Literacy with an attitude: Educating working- class children in their own self-interest* (2nd ed.). Albany, NY: SUNY Press.

Fischer, J., & Vander Laan, S. (2002). Improving approaches to multicultural education: Teaching empathy through role playing. *Multicultural Education, 9*(4), 25–26.

Fisher, D., & Frey, N. (2003). Writing instruction for struggling adolescent readers: A gradual release model. *Journal of Adolescent & Adult Literacy, 46*(5), 396–405.

Fisher, D., & Frey, N. (2013). *Better learning through structured teaching: A framework for the gradual release of responsibility.* Alexandria, VA: ASCD.

Flake, S. G. (2007). *The skin I'm in.* New York, NY: Hyperion Books for Children.

Freire, P. (1970). *Pedagogy of the oppressed.* New York, NY: Continuum.

Freire, P., & Macedo, D. (1987). *Literacy: Reading the word and the world.* Westport, CT: Bergin & Garvey.

Freire, P., & Macedo, D. (2013). *Literacy: Reading the word and the world.* New York, NY: Routledge.

Frost, K. S. (2007). *I've got a home in glory land: A Lost tale of the underground railroad.* New York, NY: Farrar, Straus and Giroux.

Gallagher, K. (2003). *Reading reasons: Motivational mini-lessons for middle and high school.* Maine: Columbus, OH: Stenhouse Publishers.

Gee, J. P. (2014). *Social linguistics and literacies: Ideology in discourses.* London, England: Routledge.

Green, J. (2012). *The fault in our stars.* New York, NY: Dutton Books.

Hamilton, J. (2007). *Date rape (issues that concern you).* San Diego, CA: Greenhaven.

Hansen, J. (2009). Multiple literacies in the content classroom: High school students' connections to U.S. history. *Journal of Adolescent & Adult Literacy, 52*(7), 597–606.

Hautman, P. (2004). *Godless* (2nd ed.). New York, NY: Simon & Schuster Books for Young Readers.

Hendricks, K. D. (2010). *Open our eyes: Seeing the invisible people of homelessness.* St. Paul, MN: Monkey Outta Nowhere

Hmelo-Silver, C. E., Duncan, R. G., & Chinn, C. A. (2007). Scaffolding and achievement in problem- based and inquiry learning: A response to Kirschner, Sweller, and Clark (2006). *Educational Psychologist, 42*(2), 99–107.

Hoffman, J., & Pearson, P. (2000). Reading teacher education in the next millennium: What your grandmother's teacher didn't know that your granddaughter's teacher should. *Reading Research Quarterly, 35*(1), 28–44.

Huber, J., Caine, V., Huber, M., & Steeves, P. (2013). Narrative inquiry as pedagogy in education: The extraordinary potential of living, telling, retelling, and reliving stories of experience. *Review of Research in Education, 37*(1), 212–242.

Hutchins, E. (1995). *Cognition in the wild.* Cambridge, MA: MIT Press.

Israel, S. E., & Massey, D. (2005). Metacognitive think-alouds: Using a gradual release model with middle school students. In S. E. Israel, C. Collins-Block, K. L. Bauserman & K. Kinnucan-Welsch (Eds.), *Metacognition in literacy learning: Theory, assessment, instruction, and professional development* (pp. 183–198). Mahwah, NJ: Lawrence Erlbaum Associates.

Janks, H. (2013). Critical literacy in teaching and research 1. *Education Inquiry, 4*(2), 225–242.

Janks, H., Dixon, K., Ferreira, A., Granville, S., & Newfield, D. (2013). *Doing critical literacy: Texts and activities for students and teachers.* New York, NY: Routledge.

Johnsen, K. (1986). *The trouble with secrets.* Seattle, WA: Parenting Press.

Klein, A. (2012). *Rape girl.* South Hampton, NH: Namelos.

Kohl, H.(2002). Topsy-Turvies: Teacher talk and student talk. In L. Delpit & J. Kilgour-Dowdy (Eds.), *The skin that we speak: Thoughts on language and culture in the classroom* (pp. 145–161). New York, NY: The New Press.

Korman, G. (2007). *Schooled.* New York, NY: Hyperion Books.

Kozol, J. (1988). *Rachel and her children: Homeless families in America.* New York, NY: Ballantine.

Kuhlthau, C., Maniotes, L., & Caspari, A. (2007). *Guided inquiry: Learning in the 21st century.* Westport, CT: Greenwood.

Kumashiro, K. K. (2009). *Against common sense: Teaching and learning toward social justice.* New York, NY: Taylor & Francis.

Ladson-Billings, G. (1995). Toward a theory of culturally relevant pedagogy. *American Education Research Journal, 32*, 465–491.

Lave, J. (1988). *Cognition in practice.* Cambridge, England: Cambridge University Press.

Lave, J. (1997). The culture of acquisition and the practice of understanding. In D. Kirshner & J. Whitson (Eds.), *Situated cognition: Social, semiotic and psychological perspectives* (pp. 17–35). Mahwah, NJ: Lawrence Erlbaum Associates Publishers.

Lave, J., & Wenger, E. (1991). *Situated learning: Legitimate peripheral participation.* Cambridge, England: Cambridge University Press.

Lee, C. D., & Smagorinsky, P. (Eds.). (2000). *Vygotskian perspectives on literacy research: Constructing meaning through collaborative inquiry.* Cambridge, England: Cambridge University Press.

Levy, B. L., Thomas, E. E., Drago, K., & Rex, L. A. (2013). Examining studies of inquiry-based learning in three fields of education sparking generative conversation. *Journal of Teacher Education, 64*(5), 387–408.

Lopez, S. (2010). *The soloist.* New York, NY: Berkley Trade.

Maloch, B., & Bomer, R. (2013). Teaching about and with informational texts: What does research teach us? *Language Arts, 90*(6), 441–450.

Mangrum, J. (2010). Sharing practice through Socratic seminars. *Kappan, 91*(7), 40–43.

McKinney, P. (2014). Information literacy and inquiry-based learning: Evaluation of a five-year programme of curriculum development. *Journal of Librarianship and Information Science, 46*(2), 148–166.

McLaughlin, M., & DeVoogd, G. (2004). Critical literacy as comprehension: Expanding reader response. *Journal of Adolescent & Adult Literacy, 48*(1), 52–62.

Melville, H. (1986). *Billy Budd and other stories* (Penguin classics). New York, NY: Penguin. (Original work published in 1924)

Mensah, P. K. (Ed.). (2010). *Defiled sacredness: A collection of poems about the effects of rape and sexual abuse on the individual and society.* CreateSpace Independent Publishing Platform.

Morgan, W. (1997). *Critical literacy in the classroom: The art of the possible.* London, England: Routledge.

Mortenson, G. (2009). *Stones into schools: Promoting peace with books, not bombs, in Afghanistan and Pakistan.* New York, NY: Viking.

Mortenson, G., & Relin, D. O. (2007). *Three cups of tea: One man's mission to promote peace one school at a time.* New York, NY: Penguin.

Myers, W. D. (2005). *Shooter.* New York, NY: Amistad.

National Coalition for the Homeless. (2006). *Facts about homelessness: Who is homeless?* Retrieved from http://nationalhomeless.org

National Governors Association Center for Best Practices & Council of Chief State School Officers. (2010). *Common Core State Standards.* Washington, DC: Authors.

Nieto, S. (1999). *The light in their eyes: Creating multicultural learning communities.* New York, NY: Teachers College Press.

O'Brien, T. (1990). *The things they carried.* New York, NY: Houghton Mifflin.

Olson, M. R. (2000). Curriculum as a multistoried process. *Canadian Journal of Education, 25*(3), 169–187.

Patterson, N. G., & Speed, R. (2007). Urban education: Moving past the myth of structure. *English Journal, 96*(6), 31–36.

Pearson, P. D., & Gallagher, G. (1983). The gradual release of responsibility model of instruction. *Contemporary Educational Psychology, 8*(3), 112–123.

Pelzer, D. (1995). *A child called it: One child's courage to survive.* Deerfield Beach, FL: HCI.

Picoult, J. (1999). *The pact: A love story.* New York, NY: Quill/Harper Collins.

Purcell-Gates, V., Duke, N., & Martineau, J. (2007). Learning to read and write genre-specific text: Roles of authentic experience and explicit teaching. *Reading Research Quarterly, 42*(1), 8–45.

Rogers, R. (2013). Cultivating diversity through critical literacy in teacher education. In C. Kosnik, J. Rowsell, P. Williamson, R. Simon, & C. Beck (Eds.), *Literacy teacher educators* (pp. 7–19). Rotterdam, NL: Sense Publishers.

Rogers, R. (2014). Coaching literacy teachers as they design critical literacy practices. *Reading & Writing Quarterly, 30*(3), 241–261.

Rogoff, B. (1984). Introduction: Thinking and learning in social context. In B. Rogoff & J. Lave (Eds.), *Everyday cognition: Its development in social context* (pp. 1–8). Cambridge, MA: Harvard University Press.

Scribner, S. (1984). Studying working intelligence. In B. Rogoff & J. Lave (Eds.), *Everyday cognition: Its development in social context* (pp. 9–40). Cambridge, MA: Harvard University Press.

Shanahan, T. (1997). Reading-writing relationships, thematic units, inquiry learning . . . in pursuit of effective integrated literacy instruction. *Reading Teacher, 51*(1), 12–19.

Shor, I. (2012). *Empowering education: Critical teaching for social change*. Chicago, IL: University of Chicago Press.

Simon, S., Howe, L., & Kirschenbaum, H. (1978). *Values clarification: A handbook of practical strategies for teachers and students*. New York, NY: Hart.

Singer, M. (2004). *Face relations: 11 stories about seeing beyond color*. New York, NY: Simon & Schuster Books for Young Readers.

Sleeter, C. (2001). Preparing teachers for culturally diverse schools: Research and the overwhelming presence of whiteness. *Journal of Teacher Education, 52*(2), 94–106.

Spinelli, J. (2000). *Stargirl*. New York, NY: Alfred Knopf Books for Young Readers.

Stowe, H. B. (1878). *Uncle Tom's cabin*. Boston, MA: Houghton Mifflin. (Original work published in 1852)

Straughtan, R. (2012). *Can we teach children to be good? Basic issues in moral, personal and social education*. New York, NY: Routledge.

Toomey, R., & Clement, N. (Eds.). (2010). *International research handbook on values education and student wellbeing*. Dordrecht, NL: Springer.

Toth, J. (1995). *The mole people: Living in the tunnels beneath New York City*. Chicago, IL: Chicago Review Press.

Tyner, K. (2014). *Literacy in a digital world: Teaching and learning in the age of information*. New York, NY: Routledge.

Van Lier, L. (2013). *Interaction in the language curriculum: Awareness, autonomy and authenticity*. New York, NY: Routledge.

Vasquez, V. (2013). Living and learning critical literacy in the university classroom. In C. Kosnik, J. Rowsell, P. Williamson, R. Simon, & C. Beck (Eds.), *Literacy teacher educators* (pp. 79–92). Rotterdam, NL: Sense Publishers.

Vitello, P. (2010, August 20). Islamic center exposes mixed feelings locally. *The New York Times*. Retrieved from http://www.nytimes.com/2010/08/20/nyregion/20muslims.html?p agewanted=all

Warner, A. J., & Myers, B. E. (2011). *Implementing inquiry-based teaching methods*. Retrieved from http://edis.ifas.ufl.edu/pdffiles/WC/WC07600.pdf

Weissmann Klein, G. (1995). *All but my life: A memoir*. New York, NY: Hill and Wang.

Weltsek, G. (2005). Using process drama to deconstruct *A Midsummer Night's Dream*. *English Journal, 95*(1), 75–81.

Winn, M. T. (2011). *Girl time: Literacy, justice, and the school-to-prison pipeline: Teaching for social justice*. New York, NY: Teachers College Press.

Woodson, J. (2010). *If you come softly*. New York, NY: Speak.

Index

An *f* following a page number indicates a figure.

About the Author

Jacqueline Darvin is an associate professor of secondary literacy education, the program director for Adolescent Literacy Education, and the deputy chair of the Secondary Education and Youth Services (SEYS) Department at Queens College of the City University of New York. Dr. Darvin received her Ph.D. in Literacy Studies in 2004 from Hofstra University and taught secondary English, reading and special education for twelve years before becoming a teacher educator. In 2002, she received the prestigious Long Island News 12 Educator of the Month Award for her work integrating literacy instruction into secondary career education courses. She was also featured in a cover story of New York Teacher, the official publication of the New York State United Teachers, for her work in Regents level, standards-based literacy instruction. She was also the recipient of the Queens College Presidential Award for Innovative Teaching in 2006. Her publications include several book chapters, articles in English Journal (the secondary journal of the National Council of Teachers of English [NCTE]) and the Journal of Adolescent & Adult Literacy (a journal of the International Literacy Association [ILA]). Her presentations include both national and international conferences on topics related to the cultural and political aspects of literacy teaching and learning.